KANYE WEST
ORE THE LEGEND:

The Rise of Kanye West
the Chicago Rap and R&B Scene

The Early Years

KANYE WEST BEFORE THE LEGEND:

The Rise of Kanye West and the Chicago Rap and R&B Scene

The Early Years

by Jake Brown

Colossus Books

Phoenix
New York   Los Angeles

Kanye West Before the Legend:
The Rise of Kanye West and the Chicago Rap and R&B Scene

by Jake Brown

Published by:
Colossus Books
An imprint of Amber Communications Group, Inc.
1334 East Chandler Boulevard, Suite 5-D67
Phoenix, Z 85048
amberbk@aol.com
WWW.AMBERBOOKS.COM

Tony Rose, Publisher/Editorial Director
Yvonne Rose, Associate Publisher/Editor
The Printed Page, Interior & Cover Design

The publication is designed to provide accurate and authoritative information in
regard to the subject matter covered. It is sold with the understanding that the Pub-
lisher is not engaged in rendering legal, accounting or other professional services. If
legal advice or other expert assistance is required, the services of a competent professional person should be sought.

Colossus Books are available at special discounts for bulk purchases, sales promotions,
fund raising or educational purposes.

© Copyright 2013 by Jake Brown and Colossus Books
ISBN#: 978-1-937269-40-1

Library of Congress Cataloging-in-Publication Data

Brown, Jake.
  Kanye West before the legend : the rise of Kanye West and the Chicago rap and R&B
scene : the early years / by Jake Brown.
      pages cm
  Includes bibliographical references and index.
  ISBN 978-1-937269-40-1 (alk. paper)
  1. West, Kanye. 2. Rap musicians—United States—Biography. 3. Rap (Music)—
History and criticism. I. Title.

ML420.W452B74 2013
782.421649092—dc23
[B]

2013020066

Contents

"We Don't Care"

Written by Kanye West

[Chorus]
[Kanye West:]
And all my people that's drug dealing' jus to get by stack ya money
till it gets sky high
We wasn't supposed to make it past 25 but the jokes on you we
still alive
Throw your hands up in the sky and say we don't care what people say

[Verse One:]
If this is your first time hearing this
You are about to experience something cold man
We never had nothing handed took nothing for granted
Took nothing from no man, man I'm my own man
But as a shorty I looked up to the dopeman
Only adult man I knew that wasn't a broke man
Flickin starter coats man, Man you don't no man
We don't care what people say
This is for my niggas outside all winter
Cuz this summer they ain't finna to say next summer I'm finna
Sittin in the hood like community colleges
This dope money here is Lil Treys scholarship
Cause ain't no to tuition for havin no ambition
And ain't no loans for sittin your ass at home
So we forced to sell crack rap and get a job
You gotta do something man your ass is grown

[Chorus]
[Kanye West:]
Drug dealin' jus to get by stack ya money till it gets sky high

Kids Sing Kids Sing

[Kanye and Kids:]
We wasn't supposed to make it past 25
but the jokes on you we still alive
Throw your hands up in the sky
and say we don't care what people say
[Verse Two:]
The second verse is for my dogs working 9 to 5
That still hustle cause a nigga can't shine off $6.55
And everybody selling make-up, Jacobs
And bootleg tapes just to get they cake up
We put shit on layaway then come back
We claim other people kids on our income tax
We take that money cop work than push packs to get paid
And we don't care what people say
Momma say she wanna move south
Scratchin lottery tickets Eyes on a new house
Around the same time Doe ran up in dudes house
Couldn't get a job
So since he couldn't get work he figured he'd take work
The drug game bulimic its hard to get weight
So niggas money is homo its hard to get straight
So we gon keep baking to the day we get cake.
And we don't care what people say
My Niggas

[Chorus]
[Kanye West and Kids:]
Drug dealin jus to get by stack ya money till it gets sky high

Kids Sing Kids Sing

We wasn't supposed to make it past 25
but the jokes on you we still alive
Throw your hands up in the sky
and say we don't care what people say

[Verse Three:]
You know the kids going to act a fool
When you stop the programs for after school
And they DCFS them some of them dyslectic
They favorite 50 Cent song's 12 Questions
We scream, rock, blows, weed park
so now we smart
We ain't retards the way teachers thought
Hold up hold fast we make mo'cash
Now tell my momma I belong in the slow class
It's bad enough we on welfare
You trying to put me on the school bus with the space for the wheel chair
I'm trying to get the car with the chromy wheels here
You tryin to cut our lights like we don't live here
Look at what's handed us our fathers abandoned us
When we get the hammers gone and call the ambulance
Sometimes I feel no one in this world understands us
But we don't care what people say
My Niggas

[Chorus]
[Kanye West and Kids:]
drug dealin jus to get by stack ya money till it gets sky high

Kids Sing Kids Sing

We wasn't supposed to make it past 25
but the jokes on you we still alive
Throw your hands up in the sky
and say we don't care what people say

Introduction

"You know what the Midwest is?
Young & Restless...
Somebody tell these N@$#az who Kanye West is!"

Many brilliant artists are dead long before their impact is recognized and legacy crystallized, or even established and explored in any analytical depth with the hindsight of the past to compare and contrast with. Beethoven died in an unmarked grave; Van Gogh cut off his own ear out of artistic frustration over a lack of acknowledgement; Edward Munch's paintings weren't recognized for their genius until well after his death. Thankfully, Kanye West is getting his due props now, in the moment, because he demands it. West wouldn't desire just to shoot for the stars, even when he was producing them, as he wanted most of all to be one in his own right.

Few realize how important Kanye West has been to hip-hop, well before he became a solo phenomenon, back when he was still a fledgling producer working on Jay Z's The Blueprint, arguably the first 5 MICs-worthy album of the Millennium, and the record which most critics and fans alike consider to be the most musically consistent and influential album of his career. Rolling Stone

Magazine pointed out that "delving further into his roots, Jay-Z deepens his sound on The Blueprint. Here, Jay-Z and his producers (especially Kanye West) turn to vintage soul, fueling almost every song with a stirring vocal sample: Al Green, Bobby 'Blue' Bland, David Ruffin and the Jackson Five, for starters."

The latter quote, in its own, was crediting the musical soundscape laying beneath Jay Z's vocals as the sonic foundation of where directionally hip-hop 's next generation was heading. Turns out, they were all 'College Dropouts' living a gritty reality that blended a healthy celebration of musical derivatives spanning the past two generations of African American music in the form of West's unique style of sped-up soul samples laid over beats that captured the moment better than any other producer to come along since Dr. Dre. It is arguable that only Dr. Dre has had a more rounded role in shaping the way the world of hip-hop has turned, and even a brief glimpse over Kanye West's production resume leaves no doubt that his musical legacy will be looked back upon and studied for its historical importance in the years to come. Take fellow hip-hop mogul P. Diddy's view on West's relevance to the future of the rap game, with Combs explaining that "God put him here to do this.

As for West's own perspective on what was to come with his sound in the context of impact, he explained that "I said this is something that is going to be around forever and will be hailed as the curve of where music should be. Imagine seeing a person who everybody said couldn't rap and going up and telling somebody that. They are going to say, 'This dude is crazy.' Now, one year later that crazy one is a genius, but genius is crazy in itself. I always say you have to be a little postal to push the envelope...I'm getting away with things that you're not supposed to be able to get away with in a record...I'm a representation of real people. I speak for what everyday people go through. I'm like a class clown too. I compare my style a lot to Dave Chappelle, but I bring up really serious issues that I might cover up with a joke so that we laugh to keep from crying."

West was the first hip-hop spokesman for the African American SUBURBAN population, those who had grown up as he did—in the blue-collar Midwest. Consider VH1's summary of West's appeal, pointing out that "the secret of West's success (is that, as a producer, he)…speeds up soul samples until Chaka Khan sounds like Minnie Mouse, and his often hilarious lyrics take on everything from the car crash that left his jaw wired shut ('Through the Wire') to his crappy summer job at the Gap ('Spaceship')."

West could rap about spending afternoons at the shopping mall, rather than on the street corners. He could rap about being a minority student in a statistically white-dominated University system where he wasn't a star athlete, rather just another student. He could rap about coming from a working class family, but with a mother who had a doctorate, but who still championed her son's career pursuits as blindly as a single, black mother working at menial labor jobs to support her children's dreams.

West had plenty of COMMONalities to the well-known story of the young, black male—from the working class neighborhood in Chicago he grew up in, to the fact he was the product of a single-parent home. The difference with West as a reflection of a specific demographic of African Americans between the ages of 16 and 25 laid in the fact that he wasn't escaping the ghetto, rather the working class. According to the United Negro College Fund, "today, 105 black colleges and universities educate a new generation (of African Americans)." As West himself reasoned, "I started doing this, I just came out confident to combat all the people who told me I couldn't make it. Then when I got on TV, people still saw that confidence, but they also saw this mild-mannered rapper dressed like Carlton from The Fresh Prince of Bel-Air, rhyming about social issues and joking around. People knew I had a fire, and they were all ready to hang that Tupac gangsta sound on me.

But when they heard my music, they were like, 'Oh, what's wrong with him? This is not what we expected.' "

Kanye West spoke for this generation arguably for the first time as a hip-hop record buying demographic. West's family had grown up outside of the projects, but not quite at the level of the middle class.

As a product of a working class home where he was expected to be the first child to graduate college, rather than merely high school, Kanye West gave that generation an identity it had not previously had. As the producer explained, "I really felt like those kids were not being spoken for. We got candidates right now, Democrats and Republicans, who try to speak for those who have not been heard; at the same time, these politicians are also trying to sell their message to the masses, so they have to back off sometimes. People ask me a lot, 'Do you feel like more brothers in music are being positive now?' And the politically correct answer would be yes. But I think music itself is a form of entertainment, and as entertainers we have choices. You can choose to be a Spike Lee and do something for the community with your art, or you can choose to make Bad Boys-type movies...But there are always leaders and there are always followers, so maybe I'm at the head of a new wave."

His was an updated profile, and much more accessible than the generic reformed-crack-dealer-turned-rap-superstar/entrepreneur. The late 1990s had already established that generation of hip-hop superstars, and it was West who both updated the sound and image of hip-hop into something still street but more reflective of hip-hop 's mid-section of record buyers. By pitching himself in image as a college student, he was targeting a largely untapped image that few if any hip-hop stars had taken on. Moreover, West was in a position as both producer and rapper to exclusively create and tailor his own sub-genre of hip-hop .

However, when West first went about trying to sell Corporate record executives on the idea that such a sales demographic even existed potentially, he found he would have to truly build his niche from the ground up, explaining that "(it was no) joke—I'd leave meetings crying all the time…It was a strike against me that I didn't wear baggy jeans and jerseys and that I never hustled, never sold drugs. But for me to have the opportunity to stand in front of a bunch of executives and present myself, I had to hustle in my own way…I used to always feel awkward around a lot of rappers. Other people came from hustling and all that. Sometimes it was harder to relate. People would look down on me for the way I dressed, because my raps weren't really that good—it was like, 'Just shut up and do beats.' "

Combating the latter, while his production style was feel-good soul samples sped up to a current relevance, lyrically he took hip-hop in some radically and wildly new and different directions on 'College Dropout' than it had been prepared to go at the time. He challenged societal boundaries with a boldness not seen since Tupac Shakur. Still, West had no interest in being a part of the thug life, rather he sought to preach and project a more mainstream message and image that was not so radical by nature, but equally as profound. Consider the topic of religion being infused in mainstream top 40 on the song 'Jesus Walks' in a time when religious divisions are at a cultural height in America. By suggesting that "I ain't here to argue about his facial features, or here to convert atheists into believers, I'm just trying to say the way schools need teachers. The way Kathie Lee needed Regis that's the way y'all need Jesus. So here go my single, dog. Radio needs this. They say you can rap about anything except for Jesus…That means guns, sex, lies, videotapes. But if I talk about God my record won't get played?" In just those few lines alone, West was challenging America to consider the question, and in doing so, the implied divisions therein.

As a lyricist, West displayed a gift from the jump for precisely calling America on its shit, in a way that was hard to make excuses for. West held everybody to account, even himself, which made him

9

that much more accessible as an emcee. Fans of any music genre want to see some of themselves in their musical idols, whether they be gangsta rappers reflecting the norms of the inner city in how it shapes its human byproducts or white suburban or trailer park kids who see their own experience projected through Eminem's lyrics and image.

Kanye West could cover multiple demographics with one broad stroke because he had a foundational sound that had an appeal as universal as good times are for everyone, and a knack for writing hits that everyone could dance to while having those good times. As the producer/rapper explained it, "I rap in such a way where the hood can respect it; but I can sit right in front of a white executive and spit the exact same verse and he'll understand at least 80% of it... It's harder to come up with simple lyrics...those complicated lyrics? Get that outta here man! The simple stuff is the hardest!...I'll take opinions from anyone from Jay-Z to a janitor, and I might value the janitor's opinion more...I want it so no one can front on it. People say you can't please everyone all the time. I don't believe that. I think you can."

In West's view, a party was a party, a club is a club—no matter how white or black or Latino it might be in terms of patrons. He made music everyone could dance to, laid underneath a message that didn't allow anyone to become a victim, which allowed it to be relative to everyone in one way or another. For instance, in 'All Falls Down', West raps, "Man I promise, she's so self conscious. She has no idea what she's doing in college. That major that she majored in don't make no money. But she won't drop out, her parents will look at her funny. Now, tell me that ain't insecure. The concept of school seems so secure, Sophomore three years ain't picked a career."

The latter is the story of millions of college-era kids caught in their early-to-mid 20s without a clue yet of what to do with their lives, but already old enough to be expected to have a good idea.

Speaking further for that generation, West speaks in 'We Don't Care' to and for those "sittin in the hood like community colleges. This dope money here is Lil Trey's scholarship, cause ain't no to tuition for havin no ambition. And ain't no loans for sittin your ass at home, so we forced to sell crack rap and get a job. You gotta do something man, your ass is grown."

West has established himself as well more than merely a role model. With the vast ground he has covered with his music and message in such a brief period of years, he falls into the category of phenomenon. From West's own vantage point in context of the aforementioned, he explained that "I like to educate people...I like to be the one that can reach people who don't like to pick up a book...Don't I have the right to write about how things are affecting people?...But rap has always had this premise that if you didn't do it, you can't rap about it. I'm more of a writer or poet than a rapper. A rapper is all about image. Being a writer, I have the right to be a person...I like to say something that might change someone's life."

Though he pitched himself commercially as a 'College Dropout', West as a producer was clearly not just a student, but rather a scholar of musical derivatives. He had matriculated—in scholastic terms—across every sub-genre from 40's crooners to 70's R&B. What critics quickly gave West advanced credit for, however, was his instinctive ability to match and mash up—or in some cases outright reinvent—a classic R&B melody or the most obscure of soul samples with beats so modern that listeners felt right in the moment. His sound was what was bumping in the car or club at that musically most carefree moment; yet lyrically, he had his finger on the pulse of every anxiety and reality his listeners were seeking escape from in his music. At the same time that he was shaping a profoundly accurate lyrical movie of life for his generation of African American listeners, West was thinking of their future with lines like 'this dope money here's Lil' Trey's scholarship.' West's lyrical reports on the state of his generation were the equivalent of a musical newscast, offering coverage of all things black—from institutional plagues in the inner city and more broadly throughout society by killing their confidence in any system besides those like Welfare. Really any system that in the long run, as West seemed to view it, only worked to hold back the rapper's race at large. Those avenues through which African Americans could make the greatest gains—sadly—were literally the streets, and largely, through illegal means.

Consider the bottom line of West's message about 'education', where the rapper/producer reasoning that "God put me in a position to bring change. I would be doing a disservice to not use this gift that I have. I started a foundation, The Kanye West Foundation to help bring changes in the school. A lot of major cities have over 50% drop out rates among African Americans and Latinos. I started a program that puts a (recording) studio in the school. When I went to school, it was for music, basketball, gym and lunch. I weathered through the other courses and graduated… High school is a necessity and these kids need every chance they can to survive because it is a hard world, just to say the least… They say, 'Go to school and your life will be perfect…I'm not sayin', 'Don't go to school.' But if you do go, know that you still have to make decisions for yourself. It's not just 'Get straight A's and your life will be happy ever after."

Further, because programs like Affirmative Action and related minority assistance and scholarship mandates were constantly under attack, or under funded if financed at all. As a result, faith in the opportunity for a college-level education was further eroded in context of the post-graduate lack of difference the degree actually made in terms of societal perceptions, which unfortunately play a great role in terms of access to the 'good life.' Consider lines like 'For that paper, look how low we'll stoop. Even when you in a Benz, you still a nigga in a coupe.'

For those who were in school, West next dealt with anxieties over post-graduate opportunities within the job market that could both cover student loans and still allow blacks to advance monetarily beyond the generation before them. As the rapper explained it, "my whole concept of life is just, you know, use school, but don't let school use you. It's so many people that go to school for three years, and they have no idea what they are doing. They're just in school because they don't want their parents to look at them a certain way. And then they end up dropping out, or they graduate but they can't even find a job in their major. Like, this nigga graduated at the top of our class; I went to the Cheesecake Factory, and he was a motherfucking waiter there… It's my past. I dropped out of school because I wasn't learning fast enough…I learned from real life better."

'College Drop Out' was the smart-man's 'Chronic', turning street knowledge into something much more modern and enlightened by even suggesting the idea that young, black males had a chance to make it out of the street. West took the generic 'stay in school' message and advanced it beyond the idea and theoretical, and into the realm of possibility. In a sense, the rapper displayed more faith in his generation's potential than virtually any rapper had before him. He wasn't speaking for the hustler-to-hip-hop C.E.O. generation as much as he was the hustler who would never make it to that level. Those who wouldn't ever own their own record label or clothing company; who couldn't rap at all, who could only listen.

Kanye West offered a voice for the average rap fan who just wanted some good music to motivate him through his day, whether hustling or working for U.P.S. For those for whom college graduation was like attaining a platinum record in the eyes of their parents' generation. For those who would only ever aspire to be part of the new African American middle class. He offered a blueprint for both the possibilities and the inherent struggles implied once the transition had been made from the street to the classroom.

Much in the way of the mentality that the street takes no shorts, West didn't offer or accept excuses either, explaining that "my job is to break down the barriers and show music is just music…On one hand, I've got a knowledge of my heritage; I got a pretty good background, I've been to school. But on the other hand, I like strippers. So do I not talk about strippers because I'm educated? Do I not talk about education because I like strippers? Nobody can pigeonhole me and determine what I talk about." He was clearly seeking to move his listeners beyond the club, out of that mentality entirely if possible, by simply pointing out that possibility existed at all.

As much as West didn't make excuses for his own people, he didn't make them either for the system that had failed them. Consider lines like 'you know the kids gonna act a fool, when you stop the programs for after school.' West's rhymes were sophisticated enough to break African Americans down beyond their statistical definitions and demographics; to recalculate and formulate the numbers (and implied chances) beyond their traditionally negative classifications. As a professor of the logic and reasons behind why those statistics added to something insurmountable for the average black, West was trying to give listeners real answers for a change.

Where the system offered excuses to keep them in the dark, West was pulling the wool back from a generation's eyes for the first time. West was acting much like an intellectual credit union, offering his listeners low-interest loans on an education, which, as an investment, yielded a much higher return, and all for the cost of a CD. For those who would put West's attempts to advance down, he offers that 'they are my motivation, my inspiration, cause we the leaders, and they the followers, we the nutt busters, and they the swallowers, they are the rumors, they are the lies, we the shit dog, and they the flies.' Perhaps he was speaking in a way to those among society at large who would suggest that things are today equal between blacks and whites. In terms of opportunities,

West suggests they are still very much denied, or discouraged at the very least from pursuing.

Though the potential is there for West's generation, according to an article in the New York Times 'Plight Deepens for Black Man, Study Warns', "Black men in the United States face a far more dire situation than is portrayed by COMMON employment and education statistics…Focusing more closely than ever on the life patterns of young black men, the new studies, by experts at Columbia, Princeton, Harvard and other institutions, show that the huge pool of poorly educated black men are becoming ever more disconnected from the mainstream society. Especially in the country's inner cities, the studies show, finishing high school is the exception, legal work is scarcer than ever and prison is almost routine, with incarceration rates climbing for blacks even as urban crime rates have declined."

In explaining why society is inherently pre-programmed to be racist even when it tries through the same corrupted system to push the concept of advancement, West reasons that "a whole part about being a human is to be a hypocrite. They say that if you're an artist you have to stand for this, and they try to discredit you. Like they'll try to discredit Dr. King or Bill Cosby or Jesse Jackson 'cause they say that they saw them with a woman or something. So what does that have to do with what Cosby's TV show meant for us, what it meant for the black image and meant for our esteem."

For as far-reaching as Kanye West's sound has potential to span, it has to first start and strike at the heart of the disenchanted, and move outward to embrace those who haven't necessarily known how to understand in the past—even SUBURBAN African Americans. By drawing a COMMONality out of struggle, West inspires the promise of progress much like a Civil Rights Leader like Martin Luther King or a President like William Jefferson Clinton have in the past, by treating African Americans as equal to anyone, rather than as someone different.

West is the millennium's first rapper with enough musical and lyrical sophistication to imply through his music's message that everyone—from the inner city to the suburban, middle-class young, black male—has the same right to go to college as his or her grandparents did to sit in the front of the bus. The parallel lies in the erasing of labels—be they colored-only bathroom signs or those more subtle ones put on display in reality TV shows.

Through his sound, West breaks it all down, and in the course of *Kanye West Before the Legend: The Rise of Kanye West and the Chicago Rap and R&B Scene,* we as students will uncover the method behind this genius's multi-platinum madness, from Jay Z's 'The Blueprint', lesson by lesson, through to 'College Drop Out' and 'Late Registration', and beyond. His beloved Chicago Times certainly felt that was the case in late 2003 when they predicted that "West is indeed really putting it down, and the answer to his question of 'what if' is that he seems destined to become hip-hop's next multi-platinum superstar."

— Jake Brown

"They used to consider me a prodigy—until I got too old to be one...There's nothing I really wanted to do in life that I wasn't able to get good at. That's my skill. I'm not really specifically talented at anything except for the ability to learn. That's what I do."

—*Kanye West*

Part 1
Kanye West on the Come-Up

Many in modern day—including the rapper/producer himself—would ask: who is more contemporary or cutting edge than Kanye West? From his name to his lyrical game, many have concluded that this super-producer/emcee *IS* the future of hip-hop . Amplifying the latter proclamation, West has boasted that "I'm the closest that hip-hop is getting to God. In some situations I'm like a ghetto Pope."

Kanye's mother, the late Dr. Donda West, further explained that "he's always been a very confident young man. I would like people to know that he can back up what it is that he is talking about. That's a gift from God. Both of us agree." If the latter is the standard for asserting greatness, Kanye had been backing it up in terms of potential for the better part of two decades, falling into the category of that one extraordinarily talented child everyone knew and was amazed by who could accomplish and excel at any subject he/she applied themselves to.

Typically, the latter versatility shows up in artistic children most obviously, be it in music where a student is a multi-instrumentalist or can play any song by ear for instance, or art students who can express themselves across multiple formats/mediums, spanning from sculpting to painting to photography, and so forth.

For West, as a child he was more a prodigy than even an above average talent, explaining that "they used to consider me a prodigy—until I got too old to be one...There's nothing I really wanted to do in life that I wasn't able to get good at. That's my skill. I'm not really specifically talented at anything except for the ability to learn. That's what I do." Aside from God-given talent, West also benefited from an early age from endless encouragement at home, explaining that "basically, my parents told me I could do anything." The producer's creative genesis began not with music, but rather with video games, with West explaining that "I never finished them, because I ended up going to the music part of it and staying there. I wanted to do everything: I wanted to design the characters, design the backgrounds. I would be studying different things and trying to come up with a new idea. It didn't compare with the games that were out there, but I was trying my best. I got to draw all the characters, then try to redraw them in the computer. It was very tedious for a seventh grader!"

Still, above all else, West's secret passion was always to be an emcee, explaining that "I've been rapping since the third grade. And in seventh grade, I figured if I want to be a rapper, I had to have something to rap over. So I started doing beats. And I really got serious around age 14, when I even charged people like, $50 for a beat here and there."

Once West had settled on rap, deciding to produce his own beats as a matter of creative pragmatism, his early influences came to include "Hurby Luv Bug, (he) might have been one of the first producers that I was like, 'Oh, that's a producer right there.' Then Teddy Riley, Full Force." In terms of artists who heavily influenced West's development as a producer and emcee, he explained that "(A Tribe Called Quest's] *Low End Theory* was the first album I bought…I was like, 'Oh sh—, [they] have whole albums? They don't just have the singles?' I was like, 'I'mma start buying a bunch of shit!' "

In context of West as an emcee, his father, Ray West, explains that "his mother and I never talked to him as if he was a kid…We always talked to him like he was an adult, and he sometimes had to catch up to the language. I'm a storyteller. I talk in analogies…I've just sat back and been amazed at where he has taken it."

West, for his own part, felt confident he was ready to be a rap star, explaining that "I thought I was going to get signed back when I was 13 years old, and come out with a record and take Kris Kross out…I'm very creative. I always want to do something different from what everybody else is doing, ever since I was little."

Recalling Kanye's musical social circle back during his come-up, fellow Chicago-based emcee and childhood friend Mikkey recalled that as Kanye got going as a producer, "I was actually the first artist singed to Konman Productions, the production company that Kanye started. He actually named me Vice President at the time, so that's really how my Rap career started…We have always helped each other, that's how it goes. There was a whole circle of us back then, such as Kanye, Rhymefest, GLC, and me. We would all work on songs together, come up with patterns or lines, and help each other overall. Sometimes we'll call each other on the phone and we'll tell each other which lines we like, or if the chorus should be reworked, things like that."

A collaborator of both COMMON and West, and early mentor of Kanye West's was local legend, producer No ID, who West recalls "(No I.D.) let me come to his crib, and COMMON had come over…(COMMON Sense's) 'Take It EZ' had just come out and I was like, 'Oh, shit! I'm finnin' to get signed!' (No I.D. told me,) 'Yo, you need to sample off of records.' When I found that out, it was all over." Underscoring the impact of No ID's influence in shaping

West's early production style, COMMON explains that "I knew Kanye since '96 and he was working a lot with a producer at the time called No ID...Kanye was coming with some good stuff, but NO I.D. was like the master at that point...The music Kanye was doing at the time was very, very good raw hip-hop ."

Another of West's prominent local and early-on influences was Doug Infinite. As West made a public reputation as an up and coming producer, privately, he was refining his skills as an emcee among his inner circle of collaborators, with COMMON affirming the latter by recalling that "I got to know Kanye. He was this young hungry like confident cat that would come around and he would always want to battle with me on the mic."

While Kanye West came up through the Chicago underground rap scene as a producer in his later teens, he graduated high school two years early, and at the age of 17, began attending Chicago's The American Academy of Art on a scholarship. Shortly thereafter, he transferred to Chicago State University as an English major. As West spent his time between the competing interests of pursuing an education and his career as a musician, he came to a realization that would crystalize his future in the music business, but also cut his college career short. The decision would play a greater role in conceptually shaping Kanye's eventual commercial break-out as a solo artist through a simple realization on the forward-seeing rapper/producer's part, in specific that "with school, I just didn't really want to be there. I was like, How do these credits apply to what I want to do in my life? So I would take courses that I could use a little bit: piano, speech, public speaking, English—which all helps me now. I had a record deal on the table back when I was 19 with Donny Ienner, (so I dropped out.)"

It was a conclusion many eventual fans would agree and identify with in context of its logic, but took a lot of convincing on the part of the biggest influence and supporter in Kanye's life, his mother—a *COLLEGE PROFESSOR*. As Dr. Donde West had originally envisioned it, "my plan was that he would get at least one degree, if not several…He said, 'Mom, I can do this, and I don't need to go to college because I've had a professor in the house with me my whole life.' I'm thinking, This boy is at it again. He always could twirl a word."

Once Dr. West had accepted Kanye's decision, she leveled her parental support with several reality checks seemingly designed to give Kanye an idea of what it felt like to earn a living with music, among other things requiring he pay $200 a month in rent, and at times, take a second job as a telemarketer and GAP salesperson. As Kanye explained, "I was still making ends meet by…doing beats. I used to charge people $250 to $500 (per) beat. I made a way just to hustle. You know, hustling doesn't mean 'Ah, you just sell drugs.'…(It means) hustle any way you can to maintain a lifestyle and then also, in all your spare time, chase your dreams. So whenever I would finish work, I would be up until 4:00 in the morning…focusing on my dream and praying for the day where I could just do that all the time."

West's two big breaks came when, within the same spread of months, he first sold a beat for $8000.00 to Chicago rapper Gravity, which caused West to believe "that's when I knew the one-year plan was out the window." His mainstream break came at age 20, when he sold a beat to Jermaine Dupri for the track, 'Life in 1472', and just months later, landed a track on Mase's 'The Movement' for the Harlem World album.

In between the two sales, he relocated to New Jersey, and began shopping his demos around Manhattan, eventually landing one in the hands of Roc-A-Fella Records A&R chief Kymbo Hip-hop Joshua, who put West in the studio one night with Jay Z. The result—six cuts off of 'The Blueprint' including 'The TakeOver', 'Where's the Love', and 'IZZO (Hova)' among others, would serve as the beginning of hip-hop 's musical reinvention as the Millennium began…

"I was born to educate and fight for what I feel is right and just. From what I can find out from being in and out of the studio, which is my first love and the love of trying to make this world a better place, God spared my life not only to do music but to use my powers to make things better for other people. He didn't put me on this planet to sell a lot of records and buy a bunch of Gucci shit... On my album I produce every track on it because I wanted to show what one creative vision would be all the way through."

– Kanye West

Part 2

Welcome to the R.O.C.

Roc-A-Fella Records, at the time Kanye West hooked up with the rap powerhouse in 2001, had been setting the trends for hip-hop since the late 1990s, principally via Jay Z's domination of the rap game in terms of sales via the Roc-A-Fella label and commercial impact on the culture at large via his Roc-A-Wear clothing line, and other relative brand endorsements. For Kanye, being linked with the label in any way, shape or form gave the producer a kind of instant credibility that established him overnight as one of the most sought-after producers in the business.

As West reasoned, being a part of the making of the 'Blueprint' was his personal moment of 'being in the right place at the right

time,' explaining that "(by working on that record), I'm part of history...Diamond D, Pete Rock, RZA, and Primo were doing (soul samples) since a long time ago. We just helped bring that style back. The beat CD I gave Jay for The Blueprint had 'Never Change'; (State Property's) 'Got Nowhere,' which would've had Sade singing on it; the joint that is now Alicia Keys' 'You Don't Know My Name'; and 'Heart of the City,' which R. Kelly initially sang on. For 'Heart of the City,' Jay came up with what he wanted to say in his head, as usual.

In the studio, the 'Fiesta (Remix)' video came on TV, and Jay walked into the booth, started recording, finished the entire song all the way to the outro, and came back in the studio. The video was still on. Those *Blueprint* records are all classics...That was the turning point in my life. Jay made all the difference...I can't say that I wouldn't have done it without him, but he made it easier because he gave me a stamp, he gave me the streets. The Roc-A-fella chain helped me get my name."

Over the next 2 years between 2001 and 2003, Kanye would produce hits including 'Izzo (H.O.V.A.),' by Jay Z, Talib Kweli's 'Get By,' Jay-Z and Beyonce's '03 Bonnie & Clyde,' Ludacris' 'Stand Up,' Alicia Keys' 'You Don't Know My Name,' and Twista's 'Slow Jamz,' among others. He additionally racked up sessions with Janet Jackson for her 'Damita Jo' album, and found time to collaborate with home-town peer and childhood friend COMMON, explaining the balance between producing superstar and up and coming artists as one in which "COMMON's project is equally as important as the Janet project. Because it's something I'm doing and I do my music for the fans. So if I'm doing a Janet I want Janet to have some shit that the people that love Janet, love this song. You know, they're like fuck that, this is what I wanted from Janet. You know, and like this is what I wanted from COMMON. This beat brings this out."

West's bar was naturally set as a producer by two important factors: 1.) the commercial level the star he was producing was at professionally, in the context of expected hits and their sales translation, and 2.) the fact that he was being hired to achieve the latter through the former, period. There was no room for second place on the charts with artists like Jay Z and Janet Jackson, and therein. West adopted the appropriate philosophy of perfectionist behind the boards in the lab, explaining that "my definition of perfectionist would be like I know I'm a perfectionist, where I'll keep working on something 'til like I don't care how long it takes until its just where it needs to be. Jay Z might take ten minutes (to write and lay down a lead vocal, and)…who's to say that, in that ten minutes, it isn't perfect? But when I hear the word perfectionist, I think of someone who burns the midnight oil."

Elaborating on what was beginning to become publicly recognized by critics and listeners as not only a clear genius, but also a musical indicator of where rap's commercial sound would almost certainly head in the coming years, its creator—West—explained that he felt all of his beats were potentially viable as commercial singles. As such, in the course of producing artists, West rarely put a creative idea to waste, often recycling a beat that didn't fit one project into something that worked magically for another, explaining that "I don't think of anything that is not radio viable…I actually produce the record up. I take like a beat that might be mediocre in comparison to some of my better beats, but I'll make like a great song out of it.

You got to think; sometimes classic songs didn't really have phenomenal beats to them. It might just be a little guitar playing, you know, and play a song to it. (An old Motown song plays in the back ground with a guitar beat) So I try to be there to an entire song. Any beat that I have, has the potential for you to make a great song of it. Alicia Keys' first single was on (Jay Z's) Blueprint with one and didn't make the Blueprint one. So at that point was I supposed to throw that beat away? I played that beat for everybody. It never left my beat CD. It finally got a chance. And now it's my greatest song I've ever done... I've ever taken part of."

While Kanye spent his days making hits for other stars, he spent nights working on becoming one in his own right. The problem West ran into repeatedly was a lack of interest on the part of A&R at most of the major labels who felt the rapper/producer moniker had been played out to a degree that made West unmarketable. As Capitol Records A&R man Joe "3H" Weinberger, who nearly signed West to a recording agreement, recalled that even after it fell through at the last minute, "Kanye was never down on himself...He'd be ready to rap on the spot, ready to tell his story on the spot, ready to make a record on the spot. He was probably the hungriest dude I ever saw. Whatever it takes. He wasn't all caked up yet, but he still had his Kanye swagger. It was definite star quality the day I saw him. He played me three songs and I was like, 'What!?' His flow was different, his beats were great, and he was performing the whole time. The energy was there, it was some real star-quality stuff."

Elaborating, West recalled, "I was producing for Jay-Z; that's how I got hooked up with the Roc. So, I was producing for J, and I was always working on my stuff since I was like in the 3rd grade. Dame heard I was going to get a deal on Capitol Records. He was figuring they were going to give me a whatever, like producer deal. Then I went ahead and played some songs and he was like, 'wait a second...its not even whack. Wait a minute...you can actually rap. Wait, no...you need to sign with us.

Kymbo Hip-hop Joshua, the A&R Manager at Roc-A-Fella, was definitely the one who changed my life, because he is one of Jay Z's best friends so he had the relationship. He was standing in the position for him to say listen to this guy right here. So he put me in position to play. And that's the most important thing—to have an opportunity for J to actually hear your shit. There are people who would kill for that…(One big misconception people had was that I worked at) Rocafella. I never worked at Rocafella. I've never been an in house producer. I just work with different artists on the Roc. Only time I was really directly connected was when I got signed as an artist."

West's signing came, in large part, by way of default, wherein Damon Dash caught wind of West's pending deal with Capitol Records after he and Jay-Z had already made the decision to pass on West as an artist. Deciding that they had nothing to lose in signing West—reportedly in part to entice him to keep producing principally for Roc-A-Fella artists, since West's star was on the rise as a producer. Former Roc-A-Fella Records Co-CEO Damon Dash recalled that "I was definitely feeling a little bit of anxiety (in signing Kanye) 'cause my man Jay-Z (was) retiring…People were on me like 'What you gonna do after this?' I personally signed Kanye, and I wanna take credit for that because I feel good that I believed in him and I saw his vision. What I didn't see was how big his vision was and how he was going to attack it himself. He's like me and Jay put into one. He's a businessman, he's an artist, and he's a producer. On a bigger level, he's positive."

Even once West was signed as the "newest member of the Roc-A-Fella team," as West proclaimed at the time, his album was put on the backburner in terms of priority. At the same time, West kept working tirelessly on the songs that would become his debut album, so much so that it almost cost him his life in a now-infamous car accident that happened on the night of October 23rd, 2002 in Los Angeles as West was driving back to his hotel from the studio.

Even while lying in a hospital bed with his mouth wired shut, recovering from multiple reconstructive surgery operations to repair a fractured jaw, Roc-A-Fella boss Damon Dash recalls that "he (Kanye) called me from his hospital bed with his jaw wired shut and asked for a drum machine…That impressed me."

Personally, Kanye recalled the details of the accident, explaining that "my jaw was broken in three places...I had nasal fractures—I'd be talking to people and my nose would start bleeding. Even to this day, I could start choking because spit will go down the wrong path. That whole area is messed up. But right now I'm healing, I'm just learning how to pronounce words like, 'What's up' with the 't' and the 's' together without it being slurred, so I can rap again...The accident was so painful...The first two or three days were like some of the worst pains in my life. I would not wish this on anybody, except maybe three people. I was scared, 'cause you hear about people dying in surgery and this (injury) is dealing with my breathing. I had so much blood coming out my mouth. Every 20 minutes I had to have one of them suction-type things. It would be so much mucus and blood...I was completely in pain and completely racially profiled and harassed (on the scene)... They did three or four tests on me for alcohol. After the first test (it should be clear) that I'm not drinking alcohol...I was sitting in the car after the accident and they kept asking me questions...I was just telling them 'I want to go to the hospital, I'm in so much pain right now. I'm gagging on blood right now.' I was just trying to breathe. Then they finally put one of them hard-ass neck braces on me, and it hurt. Then they put me on the stretcher and it was on some 'Something About Mary' shit, 'cause they dropped me and I hit my head and jaw...They wired my jaw wrong so they have to break it again and put it in the right place."

The accident's circumstances were eerily similar to those of another rising rap star almost 15 years before with the D.O.C., whose rap career had been cut short by a crushed larynx in an auto accident. The difference was D.O.C. had already released the groundbreaking 'No One Can Do It Better', giving him his place in the annals of hip-hop . As West himself explained, "I have flashbacks of what happened every day...Anytime I hear about any accident, my heart sinks in and I just thank God that I'm still here...All I kept thinking about was D.O.C., how he was in a car wreck."

Damned not to have his chances to impact hip-hop history stunted, Kanye crafted what would become his first hit in the form of a documentary about the accident in broader context of his career up to that point, and where he felt he had yet to go, amplifying the creative moment's intensity by recording the song's lead vocal track while his jaw was still wired shut.

Explaining his motivations, West reasoned that "I spit the song with my mouth still wired shut…(because I) thought that aside from it being me, that that was like some ill hip-hop shit to do. That was hip-hop to the fullest. I be like, my whole movement is hip-hop is back. I wanna just, I wanna take back hip-hop." Kanye West's accident was the personal equivalent to Tupac's being shot the first time in 1994 and going to jail even while he was still recovering in the hospital in terms of being a wake-up call for Kanye almost 10 years later.

West truly felt his career was in jeopardy, which was his artistic freedom much in the way Tupac's music was his own, motivating his signing with Death Row Records in the course of doing whatever he had to, to get out. Though West was imprisoned by a metal wire, rather than a set of prison bars, his fear and desperation were equal in terms of motivating him to find a way out of the artistic paralysis. By literally rapping through the metal wire holding his jaw together—just two weeks out of the hospital—Kanye used his moment of desperation to first show he could rap at all, let alone to show how profound his message could be in time.

Reflecting in its aftermath on the impact of his decision to record 'Through the Wire' in real time with his recovery, the rapper/producer explained that "(that song) made people care about me… There are so many superman rappers, and 'Through the Wire' made me kind of vulnerable, and the average person is like that, the average person who's in college or working a graveyard shift. I think that God spared my life to make music and to help people, to always put out positive energy. One of the reasons why I don't have a beef with any rapper or with anybody is because of the positive energy I put out. So, even if I hold myself up, I'm not putting anybody else down."

As perhaps a first glimpse into the potential West had to humanize rap for the first true time since Tupac Shakur, the song also offered a musical soundscape that paced the urgency captured in Kanye's vocals perfectly. He translated that urgency in context of his future to mean "when I had my accident, I was working on…tracks (that) were not my best work…If I would have passed that night, that would have been the end of my legacy. Now when I go into the studio, I act like this could possibly be my last day…At the point before the accident, my whole goal in life was to eventually be able to do nothing. Now that I see the type of impact I'm gonna make on music and the community, my responsibility is now to do everything for the fans, for the community."

That realization would serve as the creative framework and fabric of West's debut LP, 'College Dropout', which the producer described as "my medicine…It would take my mind away from the pain—away from the dental appointments, from my teeth killing me, from my mouth being wired shut— from the fact that I looked like I just fought Mike Tyson. The record wouldn't have been as big without the accident…I nearly died. (Commercially,) that's the best thing that can happen to a rapper."

"I feel like a lot of the soul that's in those old records that I sample is in me...So when I hear them, I put them with the drums and I bring them to the new millennium."

– Kanye West

Part 3
"College Dropout"

Kanye West is the first truly legitimate hip-hop phenomenon of the millennium. He has been almost singularly responsible for the presence of credible NEW talent to come along. With his debut LP, 'The College Dropout', Kanye West was the next generation of Biggie Smalls' Ready to Die come a few years early.

Revitalizing hip-hop in a time when Jay Z and DMX had both retired, Tupac Shakur's estate had started to run short of posthumus material from the vault, Dr. Dre hadn't released a new solo LP since 1999's 'The Chronic 2001', and Scarface had disappeared off the map almost completely. In short, there were virtually NO hip-hop heavyweights to speak of, aside from Eminem and his protégé, 50 Cent. Kanye West in essence had an open field in which to compete, with few worthy competitors, and millions of hip-hop fans desperate for a real contender to emerge.

West himself elaborated on the latter, pointing out that he's on the level he is because "before (College Dropout) came out, I talked my little shit just to let people know that there's a new dude in the

league that's running down the court talking shit, but backing it up. That's my whole niche right now. People either love it or hate it. People loved and hated Muhammad Ali. My grandfather loved Muhammad Ali and my grandmother hated him. But I bet you that more people love and remember Muhammad Ali than less. Because he used to talk shit—'float like a butterfly, sting like a bee' —and I think I say the same kind of things in my own statements. It's like, you can't please everybody, but if anybody's got a shot, it's me."

Lyrically, West took Scarface's pioneering genius for introspection, exploring vulnerability within the hardened shell of the gangsta persona, and finally for humanizing the urban experience out of the underground and into the mainstream with lyrical admissions like "we're all self-conscious, I'm just the first to admit it." By breaking down the player psyche for what it was—both in terms of the positives and negatives that the lifestyle's emphasis on material obsession with bling-bling—Kanye West allowed the listening world to see inside the mind of hip-hop through a much more honest and sympathetic lense.

Where gangsta rap had traditionally been about 'hoods' and 'sets' and keeping outsiders out, often times only allowing them access if they were music buyers, West flipped the script and sought to offer his fans unlimited access into his own insecurities as a star. In doing so, West was building a bond with his fans through an accessibility few rap stars had offered before. He made his fans feel as though he wasn't above them, but rather just like all of them in a kinship few hip-hop stars had achieved prior thereto, with West explaining that "the reason why The College Dropout went gold in its first week is because that average person that buys records looks exactly like me. So it's like, you give them all. You give them this type of rap, or this type of rap, or this type of rap, or this type of rap. It's like the whole Eminem phenomenon. The average person that buys records looks like Eminem. You know what I'm saying? Just like a regular guy. You know, the average regular guy likes jewelry, or to have a nice car if he can afford it. You wouldn't opt not to have events, or you wouldn't not go on The Price Is Right—and they say, 'You win a new Benz,' and you say, 'No, I want to drive a Nova.' Uh-uh, you f—king drive the Benz. That's what you won. Everybody wants something better in life. So I speak from that aspect for the people…Good music isn't always about being in the shower with a bunch of chicks…Human beings have many different dimensions. Nelly can fill that part of their life; it is for me to fulfill other parts."

In the course of recording his debut album, West clearly was aiming to cross over multiple demographics, explaining the conceptual side of his production on 'College Dropout' as one in which "I'm pretty calculating…I take stuff that I know appeals to people's bad sides and match it up with stuff that appeals to their good sides…It's all a matter of a turning tide." So confident was West in his potential for broad appeal, that he proclaimed, "the beats on my album are the most phenomenal beats…For the most part I'm batting a pretty good average and shit on the beats…I shoot for the stars…so if I fall, I land on a cloud…I'm a pretty smart dude. I knew that if I could rap even anywhere near the caliber of my beats, I would kill the game."

Still, Kanye was clearly and vocally defensive when it came to his skills as an emcee, explaining that "I was always rapping, and it just so happened that really phenomenal rappers started rapping over my beats before I got a chance to…That put me in the classification of a producer, but I'm a rapper from the heart…In hip-hop , people always have pre-conceived ideas about you when you're a producer who also rhymes…But one of the main things I wanna stress is that Stevie Wonder produced his own music. Prince produced his own music. Tyrone Davis and Bobby Womack—all these different people. And you don't even think about the fact that they created their own songs. So I don't see what I do as being any different."

In terms of drawing a difference between the beats he saves for himself versus those he creates and assigns to other artists, a challenging choice for any producer/artist, West explained, "I love it, man. It's the best of both worlds. I love making tracks for artists who I feel can represent my beats the right way. People like Twista, Ludacris, Jay-Z, Alicia Keys, Talib Kweli. Those artists move me. So I love making a classic track for a classic artist…As for my own songs that's a dream come true."

While West definitely sought to distinguish himself from his soon-to-be rap superstar peers as a lyricist, he didn't shy from capitalizing on the new sound he had already created in the course of his *come-up* years working as a producer at Roc-A-Fella. Recording 'College Dropout' at the tail end of recording sessions for other artists, during cancellations when the studio was already paid for, and of course, at home during every waking hour he wasn't in session with another artist, Kanye explained that "the whole…(album is exotic.) From what you heard and go to every single beat, all 16 songs, can you pinpoint a beat that's similar to what you did or that anyone else did? For me to come up with 16 original beats, it's like 'Somehow Someway' is like the third version of 'Song Cry', which is like the second version of 'This Can't be Life.' You can say that 'Encore' is the third version and the second is 'Hovi Baby', and the first of its kind is 'All I Need.' It's hybrids of the same beat. 'Lucifer' is the first of its kind. 'Stand Up' first of its kind. 'Guess Who's Back' first of its kind with the baseline and the high chords. Alicia Keys was supposed to be on The Black Album that's why it sounds so similar to Just Blaze's 'Girls Girls, Girls.' But even though I didn't do the beat….we did the beat on totally different planes…Really (originally) we were making all those beats for Ghostface. Me and Just Blaze love Ghostface so much, that's Hip-Hop's (Roc-a-fella executive) favorite rapper and one of my favorite rappers, so we were trying to make all these beats for Ghostface but just so happens we're at Roc-a-fella and Jay heard them and rapped on them (for 'The

Blueprint.') We were making all these beats for Ghostface because we got so inspired by his albums. He was the only dude coming out with something worthwhile with Supreme Clientele. I feel like I got my whole style from Ghostface. Listen to what I'm saying, I need that in print, I feel like I got my whole style from Ghostface. My whole mentality about Hip-hop. He really took it to the next level."

Elaborating on the production of 'College Dropout', West explained, "I feel like a lot of the soul that's in those old records that I sample is in me…So when I hear them, I put them with the drums and I bring them to the new millennium. It's just like God's doing that…Imitation is the sincerest form of stealing! I don't mind because I used to imitate (others), when I was trying to learn how to do it. I think it's a good way to learn how to do something. I studied music that I liked and then tried my best to emulate it…I'm one with them records right there. It's a blessing. And best believe I saved some monsters for my album."

To innovate was what West did, although as futuristic as his soundscapes were throughout 'College Dropout', surprisingly, according to West, "I don't use a computer or a lot of equipment in my studio…What do I need all that stuff for?… I don't give a fuck about equipment or technique…It is just about how it sounds at the end of the day. My claim to fame is to get the most out of the least: simplify. I go through my closet every month and give away all the clothes that I don't really love. I have a better chance of putting on something good every morning if I just have all hot shit."

Utilizing stationary equipment including an Akai MPC2000 MIDI Production Center, a Gemini PT-1000 II turntable, an Ensoniq ASR-10 keyboard, and a Roland VS-1880 24-bit Digital Studio Workstation, Kanye explained his process for building a rap instrumental as one in which "I sample (albums) at regular speed, then speed them up inside the ASR-10…I just put the pitch up on the sampler, and it will go faster. The ASR-10 is like my left hand. I can chop samples into 61 pieces without wasting any memory. A lot of old songs are too slow to rap on. So I got to speed them up to a rappable tempo…What I do is I get in the studio and I watch TV or play video games for about two or three hours and then I'll listen to samples in the back and find one that I want.

I'm gonna give y'all one of my tricks right here. I'll have eight samples playing at the same time. I take the one I like the most, (then) I find some ill drums and program them and get the basic idea, the beat up and flowing." Offering some outside insight into Kanye's brilliance in the studio as a producer, violinist Miri Ben-Ari, whose playing showed up all over the album, explained that "a major part of Kanye's success is, of course, his talent…He has a vision for things, for example, to bring live instrumentalists back to the game and create music like they did back in the day. Kanye is very open to new things; he is not afraid to think differently, to take a chance and to say his thoughts out loud."

Still, as eager as everyone was during the course of College Dropout's recording to talk about West's beat-making abilities, he seemed more eager to use the latter subject as a catalyst—in general—to change the focus from Kanye the producer to Kanye the emcee, explaining that "the best thing about the fact that I did beats is I can make the perfect plateaus for me to present information over. I make music that'll catch people's ear automatically. Then when they hear what I'm saying they go 'Oh shit, he's saying some shit right there.'"

Elaborating on the methods behind his groundbreaking lyrical brilliance, West explained that, during the writing and recording of the record, "what I did was incorporate all these different forms of rap together—like I'll use old school pattens, I come up with new patterns in my head every day. Once I found out exactly how to rap about drugs and exactly how to rap about 'say no to drugs', I knew that I could fill the exact medium between that. My persona is that I'm the regular person. Just think about whatever you've been through in the past week, and I have a song about that on my album…You know, I try to put some humor in it, a little punch line. You know I have a different philosophy to punch lines. Because people have different theory on punch lines. You know let me compare how much dope I got to how much coke I got, and what's the opportunity you got of being shot around me."

Continuing, West explained that "what people need to understand is that I don't use vocabulary words and flip them into the Hip-hop meaning, I use the literal meaning of them. Like Fugees was pop. Shyne's 'Bad Boys,' one of my favorite songs, was pop. It was very popular. Like backpackers would say, 'Pop! Oh my God, that's like Britney Spears. You're going to go pop!' No, no one likes Britney Spears more than they like Jay-Z. Who's more popular? There's plenty of people that sell more records than Jay, but Jay-Z is more popular, thus making him pop. I want songs that the popular community likes the most. That's making it pop…My mom was a teacher, and I'm kind of a teacher too. But the hood, the suburbs, MTV and BET are my classrooms, and I know how to talk to my class."

A scholar of the trends in pop music, and especially in hip-hop , as he'd spent the last 4 years helping to set them off, West felt he had his finger right on the pulse of where rap both was and needed to be going, heading into the release of 'College Dropout.' Delving into the logic behind his philosophy in the course of designing the marketing plan for his debut LP, which West essentially concocted himself, the producer/rapper explained that "(I think trends flip) back and forth. Its always the era. Like it could be Rakim, then it will go De La Soul and Tribe. Then it will be Dr. Dre, then Biggie, and then now it's coming back to more of just a regular guy. Like everything has been done on a cycle because hip-hop has been around so long. So once you get so much of a something, you are just looking for a breath of fresh air, and I saw that. I saw that

opening and I just ran to it. I was like 'Yo, if I could be the first at this, I will be successful."

Needing an impeccably produced and sonically and stylistically groundbreaking album to pull the latter off, West felt he had just that when he completed recording sessions on 'College Dropout', explaining that it surprised everybody. "It even surprised me sometimes. When I got finished with it I was like... 'Damn this is good! Maybe I messed up, maybe I shouldn't have made it this good—I should have given myself some room to grow!'...I will drive myself crazy because I am a perfectionist—because my pain is your pleasure; my obsessive compulsive disorder. Some people say that I am anal, but at the end of the day that is the reason 'Jesus Walks' has a hundred tracks of strings that play for seven seconds in a song. The eye for detail can drive a person insane."

What West put into the record in terms of self-criticism, he definitely got out in terms of commercial praise ahead of the record's retail release, which naturally helped to fuel sales. Explaining why he felt his record had universal appeal from a musical vantage point, West explained that "in music and society people tell you to pick a side...Are you mainstream or underground? Do you rhyme about nice cars, or about riding the train? Are you ignorant or do you know something about history? But I'm a person who I can do all these different things. Its like everybody is taking that fork in the road. They don't see the rainbow in the middle. And I'm about to ride that. I'm the prism. And my music comes out in colors...Music is the universal language. I try to make music to relate to people but I also try to make it in a way that'll relate to everybody with the melody and a message. People talk about my album, they talk about the rhymes, the features, the quality of the beat...My main thing that I'm pushing with College Dropout is message and melody. That I learned from watching the MTV Top 100 pop countdown. I feel every song on my album is pop."

Critics agreed across the board, namely because 'College Dropout' helped the mainstream relate to rap again, with Rolling Stone Magazine, for one example of the latter, proclaiming in its review of the album that West had "perfected...(a) warm, almost sentimental brand of hip-hop, using bright, soulful beats and melodic choruses to humanize otherwise chilly gangsters...(West's) debut as a rapper on *College Dropout* might do the same thing for Jigga's Roc-A-Fella label...West has got something to prove on Dropout... His ace in the hole is his signature cozy sound—dusty soul samples, gospel hymns, drums that pop as if hit for the very first time. He has also succeeded in showing some vulnerability behind a glossy mainstream hip-hop sheen." Time Magazine, meanwhile, hailed 'Jesus Walks' as "one of those miraculous songs that you hear for the first time and immediately look forward to hearing on a semi-regular basis for the next 30 or 40 years."

In February 2004, 'College Dropout' debuted at # 2 on the Billboard Top 200 Album Chart, scanning 441,000 in its first week, and going platinum within its first month of release. In the industry's wake (or re-awakening) following the release and instant smash success of 'College Dropout', Kanye West became the overnight phenomenon he'd always expected to become. White America loved Kanye West the way they loved Chris Rock, because Kanye was brave enough to explore social and cultural topics with the African American race and reality that it was largely inappropriate for whites to comment on. For instance, Stylus Magazine, in its review of the album concluded that "*The College Dropout* can't be readily pigeonholed as eggheaded underground proselytizing or myopic mainstream bling…If the idea of a hip-hop artist who actually struggles with his social-climbing convictions, who doesn't seem to have it all figured out, sounds infinitely more fascinating to you than just another self-insulated platinum-rap puppet or self-righteous indie-rap killjoy, then maybe Kanye's onto something more than the white picket middle ground.

Throughout *The College Dropout,* Kanye subverts clichés from both sides of the hip-hop divide, which again isn't unprecedented, but still refreshing and revelatory coming from someone who could have just as easily stood pat on his massive Midas-producer stacks. Instead, you get drug dealers less concerned with flossin' than just getting by ('We Don't Care'), and college students who realize that a degree doesn't guarantee you'll be better off than the dopeman either ('All Falls Down', 'Get 'Em High'). You find institutional prejudice in the Gap, not just in the ghetto ('Spaceship'). You find African-Americans trying to orient themselves in a wider, white world and finding out, as Kanye proclaims on the album's transcendent centerpiece, 'Never Let You Down,' that 'racism's still alive / They just be concealing it'…Most importantly, you find Kanye trying to reflect the entire spectrum of hip-hop and black experience, looking for solace and salvation in the traditional safe houses of church and family, with the domestic utopia of 'Family Business' communicating the same kind of yearning as the heavenly pleas of 'Jesus Walks' "

The Village Voice, meanwhile, concluded that "West's witty, self-produced solo debut, *College Dropout* frolics…between should and can, between playful hyper-awareness and young, willful naïveté… Built from squirrelly, sped-up vocal samples, swelling choruses and handclaps, Kanye's beats carry a humble, human air."

USA Today, for its part, vindicated West by pointing out that "after years of trying to convince industry suits that he could rap as well as produce, it turns out (West) has plenty to say…this dropout goes to the head of the class." It seemed refreshing to the world of music critics—as much as it did to everyone else—that a rapper could be down to earth for a change, and the latter sentiment ran the gamut from mainstream music critics to those writing for hip-hop mainstays like Vibe Magazine, who gave the record its highest score, and AllHipHop.com, who concluded that "new pathways are now possible for both the conscious and street corner heads that previously didn't know where this rap game was headed…(Lyrically) West introspectively waves at thematically diverse topics, tendered by a poetic flow that pays homage to his own innate hip-hop infatuation. West's approach is simply cerebral; his verse remains in tempo, yet stays varied preventing monotony. His witty punch lines are slapstick, yet unabrasive. In addition, West appeals to a broad based listener group…To its advantage, the album is conceptually uncalculated, and simply impossible to trace along a straight line. From chick-chasing on BlackPlanet to religious identity conflict, *The College Dropout* runs threadfulls in obscurity; it grabs various elements frayed from far and wide, and composes them seamlessly into, yes, musical brilliance… *The College Dropout* is a refreshing reminder of reaching success in hip-hop through humility and personality, proving that West is not just simply a producer anymore. And that is what today's sound needs; a subtle aggression that concisely drives creativity in the right direction."

For those journalists or magazines—like *The Source*—who did not give West's debut the accolades and perfect scores he felt it deserved, he became surprisingly (if you didn't know him) brash given his on-record persona, proclaiming at one point that "anyone who doesn't give (College Dropout) a perfect score is lowering the integrity of the magazine." West took particular umbrage to The Source Magazine's decision to give his debut four mics out of five, arguing that "I still feel, to this day, that The Source needs to change my score to five mics…Give me my five mics. I feel like the XXL completely showed how credible they were by saying, 'Yes, I made a mistake.'"

West's confidence was backed up by the 10 Grammy nominations, including 4 wins for Best R&B Song (awarded to the songwriter) ('You Don't Know My Name' with Alicia Keys and Harold Lilly), Best Rap Song (awarded to the songwriter) ("Jesus Walks" with C. Smith), and Best Rap Album (The College Dropout) —although he took equal issue with award shows who didn't give him the awards he felt he deserved, boasting after the American Music Awards that "I felt like I was definitely robbed and I refused to give any politically correct bullshit ass (comment). I make the music from my heart, and to be able to get 'Jesus Walks' on the radio and everything that's happening, I was the best new artist this year, so get that other bullshit out of here."

Even after winning the Grammys, while sitting at the height of his massive mountain of success, West would proclaim "I'm not finished. I'm not done yet." In offering his listeners—both fans and critics alike—a peek into what he meant exactly, West predicted that his sound would embody "what music will be for the next four years at least." Interrupting his detractors in advance, West elaborated on his logic behind making the latter statement by explaining—rather sensibly—that "you can't judge 'The College Dropout.' It's something completely different…It's definitely a classic, if I stepped aside from myself and say that. We'll see the results in the next six months, of whether it did change the game or whether it is it's own entity." While West backed up his boasts with both sales and awards among other qualifiers, his arrogance was—while not new to the rap star persona—surprisingly bold in terms of the ground it covered beyond the producer/rapper's immediate and even outer realms commercially. His statements were sweeping, and in some cases, almost demanding, which certainly seemed to put some off—especially on the critical side.

It was a contentious relationship that most felt was worth exploring, but few could ever do outside the immediate context of an interview where West could immediately respond, and most times, shape and spin the nature of his answers superficial enough to keep the focus off any substantive analysis of what was underlying his apparent need for such massive praise.

The latter examination arguably is warranted considering the possibility both that West could be right, or that he could be wrong. It seemed to cost West very little either way to make the statements he did as he continued to insulate himself from criticism with award after award, week after week of consistently healthy album sales, even though any media consultant—by normal standards—would surely have advised him to tone down his taunting rhetoric to the critics, ever so slightly.

"I'm asking you all, I'm begging you all, if y'all feel this is a zero, give it a zero. If you feel like it is a five, give it a five. If y'all believe that this is the future, which is what I believe...If y'all feel like this is what the game needs right now, if y'all feel I delivered what y'all been waiting for, then...I'm asking you all not to let the future pass you by and be a part of history, 'cause this is history in the making, man...Don't you love it, though? What happened to the Muhammad Ali's and the rock stars in the game?"

– Kanye West to MTV on his 'Arrogance'

Part 4

Arrogance or Brutal Honesty?

If you'd read any of Kanye West's bold statements regarding his music without actually listening to any of it, you might conclude the producer had a massive chip on his proverbial shoulder due to some kind of past-tense rejection that was still haunting him in some way; and you'd probably be right in one way or another. In the face of being called 'Arrogant', anyone who took a look beneath his hype could see West was—in many ways—reflecting a well-earned confidence in his work product. Explaining that "arrogance (is) the steam to power my dreams," Kanye's confidence was, in ways, on par with the volume of people who were putting their faith in his music by buying as many records as they had, and embracing his sound and message as widely as the

industry and hip-hop culture overall had. Perhaps then his confidence was properly adjusted, and not out of line with the reality of his impact upon commercial hip-hop culture.

Still, some would argue that West's outbursts or rants at critics of his sound were borderline—if not outright—emotional, due to the fact that West seemed defensive about any little criticism, without realizing, in the process, that at least some of that criticism was reactionary to the extremity of some of his declarations. One popularly convenient instance being his statement in 2005 that there would be a 'major problem' if he wasn't given certain Grammys, or another more recently that magazines should pay him to appear on their issue covers. Such statements were certainly new—even to the ears of hip-hop fans—who were desensitized to hearing anything that could arguably contain shock value—at least in terms of the content of a song or record. West had succeeded in giving everyone new things to think about with his music and message; so, perhaps he was therein entitled to additional recognition or consideration come award time.

As far as the media had traditionally been concerned, a reciprocal relationship had always existed between celebrities and the press wherein the stars posed for the cameras in exchange for the implied national and often international coverage, and therein additional fame or notoriety that came with that exposure. If anything, West was uncompromising with his continual insistence that the media acknowledge his excellence on the level that he himself did. By West's logic, for instance in addressing his tag of 'arrogance' by certain journalists, "when other people say it, then it's ok; but when I say it, I'm arrogant—like I haven't been working at this since I was twelve years old. I'm 27 years old now I've been through nervous breakdowns trying to sell my beats. And now that they're good enough that I can say it's hot—everyone says 'Oh he's arrogant.' "

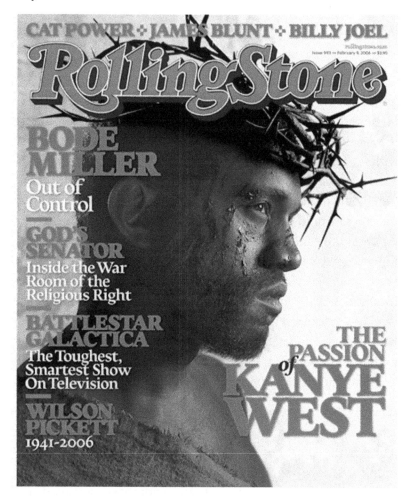

Elaborating on the reasons behind the frustrations that often inspired his controversial statements in the press, West further explained that "(there's) still a lot of disrespect at the label, though. Like, just yesterday, I wanted to book studio time to work on a song, on my album. I still have, like, over $100,000 left on my budget, that I didn't go over budget. And they wouldn't even book the studio time, because they didn't understand exactly what I was going to the studio for. And that's what happened with 'Through The Wire' a long time ago. At that point, when they did it, I am ready to just really black out. So a lot of times when people say, you know, 'Kanye seems arrogant' or 'He seems crazy,' or whatever…think about it. I am an artist that has shipped 1 million in one day. Don't you think that I should get studio time? So my thing is, just come on, man. Stop playing. Should I please be creative, you know? And the thing is, if you all won't book it, I will book it myself. And I just get reimbursed. But why do I have to keep on going through that? And it's funny. Because people will think, 'OK, now Kanye has the number one record in the country. He is just on top of the world.'

But I still go through struggles. I don't know if these people have vendettas where they don't want me to win, or if they don't want this style of music to be where it is. They don't want to accept anything new. Maybe I don't look intimidating enough for them to even respect what I am saying in the first place. I don't know what it is. But my thing is, when it comes to my music, I am so serious. I don't want anybody to comment on it. I don't want anybody to ask me what type of song I am making. I'm a true artist. I don't need no A&R direction like that. Artistry comes from me. I am walking around with my people who know real-life situations, and I am playing to the music. And obviously, it's worked now. So can you shut the hell up already?... I sat back and learned a lot from working on Jay-Z's project, from working on Ludacris, Alicia Keys...I saw things that they dealt with. And that's another reason why I won't take as much sh-t as a new artist, because I see the shit that Jay wouldn't take."

Looking beyond the surface, in certain ways, Kanye West's teflon psyche is parallel to that of an athlete who was shorter than the average player and had to run a little harder, but had more raw talent than most of his teammates. The number of rejections West got as an emcee from labels—including at first his own, Roc-A-Fella—is perhaps analogous to Michael Jordan getting cut from his sophomore basketball team.

The rejection only fueled his ambition, driving his dreams to places where only superstars can hang, and West was a bonafied

superstar by the time he'd begun making the aforementioned controversial statements. On the other hand, where in the press he was bold, brash and extremely confident, on his albums he would reveal, by his own admission, that "I'm so insecure…I say in my songs…So a lot of times, arrogance is to combat insecurity. So in order for me to go out and do what I've done, facing insecurity and facing people telling me I couldn't do it, I had to build a force field around myself." The latter was—at the very least—a much more likable answer in context of its humility, and in contrast to the boastful tone he often took in interviews, although West could reasonably argue on some levels his statements were reactionary—albeit to magazines and award nominating committees not going along with what West saw as his due praise.

Still, in some cases, he put himself out there for such analysis—whether it resulted in favorable or adverse conclusions—by admitting that "I think I've got a lot of growing to do…I've got a lot of energy. I'm growing and growing every day, and I'm finding out ways to wear my success with more dignity. The younger you are, the newer your money is, the more ignorant you're gonna act. I need to learn and have the opportunity to be around people like Quincy Jones and Oprah Winfrey." Such admissions make West much more likable and accessible, rather than so insulated from criticism that he becomes inapproachable past an inevitably superficial point.

People have always appreciated honesty in their public figures, not so much in terms of credit they feel owed, but more in terms of vulnerabilities that people can find COMMONality with. As this was clearly a goal of West's within the context of his raps, many journalists likely deduced he also sought it in the interviews he did to establish a non-musical counterpart to his on-record persona. With West seeking to walk a line, he was only human where he slipped up, and admitted as much when he conceded to one journalist that "alot of times I get frustrated, because I'm scared (and) I don't think I could do it again…My (future) is in God's hands. If

He wants me to make another album, then he'll give me the inspiration to do so. I can't force it… Man, I'm worried I'm going to fall off any minute, that I'm going to wake up one morning and just be wack—you know, lose my magical styles and shit. When I go into the studio, I pray to God before I get in front of the keyboard that everything comes out decent."

As Kanye's success grew, however, so too did his defensiveness seem to, with West claiming at one point that "people at any given time are trying to discredit my talents in some way. I've been through too much. I been through A&R's completely shitting on me, when I am about to get kicked out of my apartment. I'm trying to make it in the game, but I can't get a deal for anything, because I'm a producer and nobody will buy my album. I been through it."

Perhaps West was rejected so many times because his listeners were afraid of what he had to say. West is arguably the most outspoken rapper since Tupac Shakur, which makes the latter assertion not that much of a leap to believe. 'All Falls Down' is the Millennium equivalent of 'How Do You Want It.' Hip-hop in its perfect moment: mirroring the concept of art imitating life and life imitating art into a musical context where both could actually exist in the same time. Consider the observations alone that West makes in the song: 'the people highest up have the lowest self esteem', and 'single, black female addicted to retail' among other admissions. In fact, no one had had those kind of balls before in rap—to decisively call rap culture on their contradictions. Ice Cube and Tupac opened the door, and have given a glimpse, but West caught hip-hop with its pants down in terms of the latter. He EXPOSED something that wasn't necessarily a well kept secret, but at the very least, something White America would NEVER dared to have explored.

Meanwhile, over the years prior to West's entry into hip-hop , the reality of the aforementioned contradictions built up as rap as a commercial entity, until West's album finally forced it to all boil over. Perhaps some of his admissions stung, or some felt West was giving right wingers ammunition they didn't deserve? Still, West was the first to wear the cross in public, to take the heat and the criticism, and to reply—at the very least with consistency—in defense of his message.

As time went on, he got on more solid footing with his rationale for being so bold, focusing less on the personal side of his story in terms of dues paid, and more on the merits of why the claims that had first tagged him as 'arrogant' were in fact suspect, and that it was the industry itself who was arrogant to begin with for making him point it out. Take for instance, a more thought-out, less sound-byte framed explanation for why Magazines should pay performers in general to appear on their covers, with West reasoning that "the thing is at the end of the day magazines are doing what they are suppose to do which is entertain people. So I can't try to take them away from their jobs, my only request as an artist, is we get paid for entertaining. Why don't we all get paid at the same time? It is supply and demand.

Why would you pay me for an interview right now and I am everywhere, except for the fact that I am not a cliché bite his tongue, politically correct house nigga…These magazines make money from ads and subscriptions. But I know that part of what drives subscriptions and ads is who these magazines put on the cover…So if you're putting me on the cover and people are buying your magazine because of me, why shouldn't I get paid to be on that cover? You are going to have to pay me to do magazine covers now!…For what we give in the videos and the album, I am in the hole with College Dropout. The money does not compare to its impact it had on the world. The reason for its impact is I made it with the intention of making a quality product."

In terms of why he feels he deserves to be among hip-hop 's commercial elite in the first place, West explained that "I can call it…I say what I'm going to do and then I do it. If I said I was going to do something and it didn't happen, I wouldn't be arrogant, I would just be wrong. But since I say I'm going to do it and then it happens, then I'm arrogant…Both of my parents are teachers; I can't help but want to tell somebody something they didn't know. And there's something about this moment in time that I have to take advantage of: When I talk, people really listen." Ultimately, the debate over whether West's statements are controversial on the merits of their substance or because of how loudly he stated them to begin with became mute because the impact was favorable to Kanye. He won his Grammys, and his demand only went up, suggesting that people wanted to hear what he had to say, and beyond that, were in fact listening to a message that had a unique resonance for his generation.

"Music isn't just music. It's medicine. I want my songs to touch people, give tem what they need. Every time I make an album, I'm trying to make a cure for cancer, musically."

– Kanye West

Part 5
Kanye West: IN-DEMAND

In between the release of College Dropout and Kayne's follow-up LP, 'Late Registration', he had little time off. In much demand as a producer, West clocked time in the studio with a plethora of collaborators, ranging from John Mayer to an idol of West's—P. Diddy—for Puff's next solo LP. For Diddy, who by 2005 was the biggest star left on his label roster—landing West as a producer was a winning lottery ticket, and Diddy's best shot at becoming relevant again as a MUSICIAN to a whole new generation of hip-hop listeners who, at this point, were more familiar with Diddy for his SeanJean Clothing Line than for his music.

It was a creative pairing that Diddy described as "a dream come true for me—to be working with him. As a producer, it's really hard to find somebody that you can trust yourself to be produced by, so it's like the ultimate respect for a producer to call on another producer. I knew that he was focusing on his label and everything and he wasn't really doing a lot of outside work, (but) I called him (because) I wanted to really make sure, for my last album, that it's

one of the best. I was interested in being produced and taken to another level—a place that maybe I'm not thinking about. But I knew that at least it was with somebody that I respect, admire and love what he's bringing to the game…So I called him up, saw him a couple of times, and we had meetings. It wasn't just no passing-by thing—we had serious meetings, talked creatively.

This is my fourth day in the studio and it's been incredible to see him work. I call him boy genius, little Quincy Jones. It's like this is what he was born to do… I've been blown away… It's a blessing for me to be doing this, and to know that you've inspired somebody that also inspires you. That's really why I'm here, because I respect what he's doing. When I produce, I have a team and I orchestrate it; I don't think he knew that was what I was doing. And for him being able to do all of that is a lot. And for me to see it—seeing is believing—he's making like four or five songs a day… To be honest, you don't go into it like you're in search of something—like you know what you're going to do. You're trying to find that masterpiece, that rhythm. (I've been) doing it for so long, going on for like 12 joints, 12 years. The reason why this is my last album is I don't want to overstay my welcome. Of course I'm gonna still be doing music, but as an artist, I wanted to make sure that I was looking extremely pretty: that I can still dance my ass off, that I wasn't stiff, that when I go up and accept my awards that I still have that gleam and that shine. I feel like right now is my time."

Diddy's decision to pick West as his principal producer was yet another validation of Kanye's status as the hottest thing happening in hip-hop at the moment, and in the same time an acknowledgement that his production stamp was almost Midas in terms of what it could do to potentially revitalize Diddy as a commercial musical entity. In spite of Kanye's own personal excitement, West had little to lose from the collaboration professionally where he could have been taking a great risk in some industry insiders' eyes in context of Diddy's relevance musically, at that point.

The latter did not seem to be a motivation driving West one way or the other, as he likely first felt confident he could answer any detractors with hit records, and would likely have been therein that much more motivated by the challenge. But moreover, West held Diddy high on a personal level in terms of what Kanye clearly felt Diddy had done to innovate hip-hop beyond just the musical realm and into the commercial as an entrepreneur. By first connecting the two worlds, Diddy was a sort of capitalistic icon for those in the rap world like West who had true potential to be an heir to that throne in time.

As such, according to West, when he first got the call from Diddy, " I told him: This is a job that I had to come and do. I used to dress like this nigga. I used to study his albums and I'll try to program like them, play strings like them, and find samples like them. But little did I know that he had about eight people (producing.) So when I come in and play my beats they say, 'Man, that sounds really finished.' I was like, 'It's not supposed to sound like that?' So now I'm basically in the studio because I didn't know that you were supposed to have a string player and all that. It's not like I'm trying to bring him into my world, but a piece of my world is his world because I'm like a distant protégé of his... Man, (we're working on everything) from slow flow to uplifting to stuff that feels good for your soul, to joints where you just hear the melody and you scrunch your face up. Everything that I give them is stuff that people can just pull up and find it at a club. I'm not giving them no guilty pleasure songs—like when you have 'NSYNC in your iPod but when somebody else is in the car you play some Jay-Z or something. You can play this stuff no matter who's in the car."

Reflecting how in-demand West actually was as a producer, Diddy acknowledged that "I just get a couple of days (with him)...That's part of the deal. He's heavily in the studio and to be honest, the way he pumps out heat, he got enough heat for everybody."

Taking Diddy's circumstance in terms of commercial stakes as an opportunity to shed some light inside his own mind as a producer—outside of the spotlight as an artist—Kanye revealed some fascinating insights into his philosophy and methodology in the studio in general. Beginning with his sense of responsibility to the artists he's working with, West reasoned that "I'm just a vessel. When I go in to work on a beat, it's my responsibility and if someone gets a great record that can change their life, that can make things happen for them—it's all in God's plan. If I go and for some reason it doesn't work or this sample doesn't work—that's not what God wanted for them. I'm here to provide blessings through my music. So, I can't be selfish with that, because he blesses me in return, regardless."

While the latter largely answered the question of which beats West keeps for himself versus gives away to other artists when working in the lab, it raised another in terms of his approach to dealing with other superstar artists in terms of their own artist egos. For instance, how far can West push an artist who has a trademark or established way of working or style of rhyming?

To answer that and related questions, West explains that he tries to remain creatively flexible, such that "it depends on how the artist works. I can go from all the way, from the artist saying just play the beat and let me do everything else, to producing it all the way, every idea to even coming up with lines for artists. The thing is I'm an artist." West was truly in the midst of a creative renaissance, a jack-of-all-musical-trades who had a well of talent deep enough to share with anyone who he felt was worthy of being a part of his movement. His collaborations in turn ranged from Lauren Hill to John Mayer, and everyone in between, spanning all genres of popular music, proving West's talents as a producer were boundless.

"There's nothing that they would love more than me to come sub par so they could find something wrong...I'm not putting nothing out unless I can talk my shit. I want to give y'all something that y'all will remember... How ill is it to have someone that talks that much shit and then backs it up?"

—Kanye West

Part 6

G.O.O.D.

Maximizing on his moment, Kanye—after showing the most promise to become Roc-A-Fella's next superstar after Jay's retirement—followed the company's formula in that direction, launching a clothing line—Mascott—(including his own Tennis Shoe brand), a religious-themed jewelry brand in partnership with Jacob the Jeweler, and of course, his own record label, called "Getting Out Our Dreams (GOOD)." Proving he was willing to break with the mold and again exemplifying his sense of total independence from the norm, he did not seek to follow the pattern of Eminem and 50 Cent, both of whom had signed label deals of their own through Dr. Dre's parent company, Aftermath, ultimately distributed through Interscope, translating into a smaller piece of the pie for both, once profits trickled back down at year's end to both artists.

In West's case, just as he hadn't signed exclusively with Roc-A-Fella as a producer when he'd first hooked up with the powerhouse, he kept it strictly business with G.O.O.D., signing with Sony Music instead, with whom he'd also struck an independent production deal. Resurrecting the career of childhood friend and underground Chicago legendary rapper COMMON, and launching that of R&B newcomer John Legend, West was also going against the prototype for most other successful artist-run labels, like Roc-A-Fella and Death Row Records among others, whose artist-rosters had been almost exclusively rap by genre. The label also provided West another mechanism by which to influence hip-hop 's musical direction with the signing of COMMON, while in the same time allowing him to affect separate genres entirely with his sound via the signing of R&B singer/songwriter John Legend.

Elaborating his label philosophy, West explained he was initially reluctant to start a record label, doing so almost by default of industry norms, admitting that "I didn't even want to do the label thing...I just did it to give people the opportunity to get their dreams out. That's why it's called Getting Out Our Dreams. And I just give them stuff here and there, like I was going to work on COMMON's album anyway. Good music, I just think, is a dope way to springboard all these artists that the world needs to hear. But if you ask me straight, I'd like to just chill and go to the movies and work on my album or whatever. I'm not really on (the label) like that."

As the (rise) of any phenomenon almost always has a snowball effect, West seemed to be just rolling with it, buying into the notion—at least in part—that the label was yet another inevitable extension of his naturally belonging in a dominant position in hip-hop at that point in time, reasoning that "I think everything what me and COMMON do, everything that John Legend does, everybody that's a part of (my label) G.O.O.D. Music, we innovate along with giving you things that give you that nostalgic

feeling…Whenever I like an artist, I just want to enjoy it, I just want to be a fan…We have a good time making the music and Getting Out Our Dreams (G.O.O.D.), people can get on their computers and write anything they like, but for the most part, sit back and fuckin' enjoy it. You can't beat it, you might as well enjoy it. Anything that's hot, I'm associated with it."

"With fellow Chi-Towner Kanye West behind the boards, COMMON returns with his sixth and perhaps best effort to date, BE. Like a train ride through the 'hood, the concise, 11-track opus steamrolls through the images, stories, and emotions of urban folks getting by any way they know how. Overflowing with passion, honesty, and optimism, BE gets to the root of human experience—all the while staying beautifully soulful and funky. The lucid block imagery and stripped-down beat of BE's first single, 'The Corner,' sets the raw, back-to-basics tone for the rest of the album. Pounding drums and a sparse bass riff open up space for COMMON to fire away photographic descriptions…

For all of BE's poignant moments, the largely '70s-laced production keeps the album triumphant and head-nodding throughout.

Jay Dee drops wicked drums and a chopped Marvin Gaye vocal sample on the warm and fuzzy 'Love Is.' Kanye stretches a trumpet note over a twisting wah-wah guitar and record-scratching on the battle song 'Chi City,' prompting COMMON to shoot off venomous punch lines. Heavenly vocals from G.O.O.D. Music family member John Legend and neo-soulster Bilal lift 'Faithful's reflection about the guilt of cheating on a woman, while the cozy electric keyboard runs, crisp snares, and hungry verse from forever-young rapper Consequence keep the vibe of 'They Say' upbeat and authentic...If anything, BE gets docked for COMMON's recycling of topics and lyrical tricks (we're familiar with the pedophilic uncles, children of a lesser God, and juxtapositions 'between this and that').

KANYE WEST
PHOTO GALLERY

In The Studio

*Kanye West In the Studio with the legendary Rick James and Rapper Bump J
(Rick James passed away a month later on August 6, 2004)*

Kanye...With Mom

Kanye…With Friends

...and Fans

Kanye...Speaks Out

Kanye...
ON Tour

Kanye…Winning Big
(Grammy Awards)

Vibe Music Awards

Billboard Music Awards

BET Awards

NAACP Awards

TRL Awards

Brit Awards

Kanye...Performing

Kanye…
Taking a Quiet Moment

KANYE & KIM

"COMMON's album is so good that I feel like we have reached a new plateau in hip-hop: COMMON's album is as good, if not better, than The College Dropout."

Kanye West

Part 7

COMMON & John Legend

West's decision to start a record label showed off his ear not only as a producer, but by extension as an A&R man, beginning with the COMMON sense decision to sign Chicago rapper and childhood friend COMMON, whose debut LP, 'BE', was released on May 24th, 2005, and quickly went platinum. Recalling the history that provided the roots of their artistic and commercial collaboration and partnership, COMMON recalled that one was almost a natural outgrowth of the other, such that "I've known Kanye for nine years...First of all, I believe that Kanye is from the same womb of music that I am. He loves the Tribe Called Quest's, and the Pete Rock's, the DJ Premier and Gang Starr stuff, that's probably his home too. But he's been blessed to do other sounding music also. So, when we started working, I think he was at home with it and I did challenge him to grow from that route—that way. 'Cause I wasn't goin' any other way. I did challenge him to grow as a producer, he challenged me to grow as an artist, as an emcee."

Elaborating on the roots of their artistic come-up together, legendary Chicago producer and mentor to both artists NO ID—who also produced COMMON's first two albums—explained that "Kanye would beg to give COMMON beats…But Kanye made Puffy-style popish beats, so COMMON would be like, 'Nah, I ain't messing with him. Don't have him come around.' Back then, COMMON didn't want input. And, you know, Kanye is very 'Let me help.'"

Recalling, for his part, that a healthy competition existed between the two rappers on the come-up, West recalled that "he thought I was, like, a New York dickrider 'cause I used to rap just like Raekwon and Nas…But he knew that I had a spark lyrically, otherwise he wouldn't have let me battle him…I used to love people like Wu-Tang Clan, Biggie, and Nas—people that sold records…I liked COMMON okay, you know, since he was from Chicago, but I wanted to dress like Nas."

For COMMON's part, he summed up any artistic rivalry as "just Kanye trying to prove himself…But it was all in fun…I got to know Kanye when he was this young hungry like confident cat that would come around; and he would always want to battle with me on the mic. I have known him for a minute, but we never got up on any music. But, we got together at the right time because his was vintage music for me to lay my rhymes down and we made good songs."

By 2004, the two had gotten on the same page artistically, with West realizing he had an untapped superstar waiting in the wings with COMMON, and quickly acting to make the rapper the first signing to his G.O.O.D. label. Justifying why the pairing worked as well as it did in the studio—an acknowledged departure from prior attempts on West's part to work with COMMON—the latter emcee explained, "Kanye and I are from the same womb of music as far as the soulful dusties, along with the hip-hop. Some of his favorite music in hip-hop was A Tribe Called Quest and

Pete Rock and De La Soul, and that's some of the same music I grew up listening to and really appreciating. We definitely come from the same place, even as far as our similar backgrounds growing up. But one thing I have been noticing about how we balance each other out is that Kanye is more outgoing and overt about his confidence."

Putting his own confidence in West as a producer was easy for COMMON, once the two had reunited in 2004 to begin work on what would become BE—which West produced 9 cuts for. COMMON elaborated on their creative process in the studio by explaining that "Kanye and I would sit in the studio and listen to music…He would find a sample that he liked and start cooking it up, and I would either be like, 'Oh, my God, I can't wait to write this!' or 'Kanye, that's cool; let's go to the next one!' On some days, we would get three songs that I would end up not using, and on some, we'd get two that ended up on the album. The music he was creating venerated what I wrote…We made this music together we were both hungry and excited and we did what we were proud of. He is an honest dude on how he feels like, he may say I can freak this verse up or I was honest like we need a better beat for this but it all came together like fam. It has a timeless feel to it you should be able to play this years from now…(Also), I got to attribute a lot to Kanye too. He pushed me as an artist. He made music that was incredible… that was me, but the masses could still touch down with it. He came with ideas and choruses so I got to give him credit, man. The dude is definitely a genius."

Financially speaking, COMMON also recognized the obvious benefits via signing with WEST, of jump-starting his mainstream career on the back of Kanye's own successes commercially, explaining that "not only do I love Kanye creatively and as a brother…but we doing business with a vision…This is the first time that I've been part of a movement where we're doing business together; and we're making each other wealthier. I used to always create music, within a movement, that would stand; but we never had the economic structure together. This time we have the economic structure. ('BE' will) bring more money into him and for myself…His success opened people up to new music and people in hip-hop that were doing something that was like humanity. Talking about spirituality, talking about they flaws, talking about they desires. Talking about having fun and being creative. It opened people up to that the music I've been doing—that brand, that style of music. Kanye had his own sound, but I'd been doing something in that vein for the longest time. Kanye was needed to open the doors, man, so the masses could enjoy it and then say, "Hey, this is a good sound," and we do love other things besides just guns and bitches and whatever things hip-hop was only showing. He was the catalyst, the spark. He opened a whole new side of hip-hop back open. A lot of hip-hop artists that were doing the conscious music—it had never reached the plateau that Kanye had reached. He took it to another level…I think Kanye issued in a new era in hip-hop and he also just allowed people to see that you don't have to be gangster, you don't have to be super eccentric to be creative and be good. He allowed people to really appreciate the raw, soulful hip-hop artist and he really opened a lot of doors for us."

Vibe Magazine's Review of COMMON's 'BE' stated, "Some will argue that lines like 'I stand for the blue collar' are self-righteous. Still, he more than makes up for these banalities with his evolution from a 40-toting street poet to an earthy soul child to a dynamic artist. Yes, COMMON Sense is back and better than ever. Grab a plate, and feed your mind, body, and soul."

For West's own part, after COMMON's album topped platinum sales, the producer/rapper seemed to take the album's success as yet another sign that rap was heading in the right direction under his own creatively and commercially, explaining in context of COMMON's success that "I'm feeling good about hip-hop right now. We went in and worked on that album—we didn't make a cookie cutter album. Every beat we made from scratch and cooked up especially for COMMON, every chorus was thought out. All type of good songs was kicked off the albums to narrow down to the eleven that you got…COMMON's album is so good that I feel like we have reached a new plateau in hip-hop: COMMON's album is as good, if not better, than The College Dropout."

John Legend and Kanye West's genesis as a creative duo began in the course of producing College Dropout, contributing as a vocalist, pianist and co-writer on several of the album's cuts. Legend, much like West made his come-up as a producer. West was already a well-established name in the industry as a songwriter at the time Legend signed with West, having previously found success co-writing hits like Alicia Keys' 'If I Ain't Got You', Janet Jackson's 'I Want You', as well as collaborations with artists including Jay Z, Lauren Hill, Britney Spears, Eve, and COMMON, among others.

The latter collaborations helped to shape his own artistic identity on the outset of entering the studio with Kanye to produce his debut for G.O.O.D., 'Get Lifted', with Legend reasoning that "experience is a great teacher. I've had the honor of working with some of the greatest artists in black music, and I can't help but be a better artist as a result of it…Clearly, it gave me a lot of experience working with great artists on classic albums…Anytime you get that kind of experience it will rub off on you. I learned to make the best of those opportunities, and it helped me to make my project better."

Introduced to West through his roommate, Legend explained the genesis of his and West's creative partnership as one in which "my college roommate Devo introduced me to Kanye. They are cousins. Devo is a producer, too…He kept telling me that I needed to meet his cousin and that we should work together. I was performing around the NY area pretty regularly, and Kanye came to see me perform at one of my shows. From there, we started working on tracks together and have been doing so ever since."

For West's own part in explaining why the pairing was as mutually beneficial in a creative sense for West as it was for Legend, the producer/rapper explained, "John Legend is just ridiculously talented. He's an extension of my style and shit, and I'm an extension of his. We just work together so much in the studio, we have such a good working relationship. You know, and he's got the image…I like the way people's voices sound, their real voices…Your voice has to be incredible…What you represent has to be incredible. That's the reason, I guess, this…(album) sounds so incredible 'cause these are the real artists, the artists that mean something to the world in their own right."

Initially in their collaborations together in the studio, Legend served primarily as Kanye's 'hooks' man, singing on choruses for Jay Z's 'Encore' and West's likely more famous 'Jesus Walks.' At the same time, he explained, "I was getting turned down by labels with the album that I am now releasing…I guess timing is important. So the timing worked out, and it is all good. We re-recorded everything and finished the album."

Released on December 8th, 2004, 'Get Lifted' debuted at # 4 on Billboard's Top 200 Album Chart, and topped the Top R&B/ Hip-Hop Albums chart in January of 2005. Quickly going platinum, the record also produced the smash 'Ordinary People', which many credit with revitalizing R&B in its own right.

Peaking in the Billboard Top 100 Singles Chart top 10, the single was certified Gold later that year. In August of 2005, Legend was nominated for 3 MTV Music Video Awards, including Best Male Video, Best New Artist, and Best R&B Video, all for the aforementioned single.

In November, Legend was also nominated by the American Music Awards for Favorite Soul/R&B Male Artist, and in February, 2006, cleaned up at the Grammy's. Legend won 3 Grammy Awards for Best New Artist, Best R&B Album (Get Lifted), and Best R&B Vocal Performance—Male (Ordinary People), and was

nominated for Song of the Year (awarded to the songwriter), Best R&B Song (awarded to the songwriter) ('Ordinary People'), Best Traditional R&B Vocal Performance ('Stay With You'), Best R&B Vocal Performance by a Duo or Group ('So High' with Lauryn Hill), and Best Rap/Sung Collaboration ('They Say' with COMMON and Kanye West).

Legend's wins were further validation for West, who somewhat humorously remarked following Legend's awards that "I would have been more disappointed if I didn't have a good performance and I had won Album of the Year…I'm happy, because I have accomplished so much in the last two years, all the way from running the (G.O.O.D.) label to being the artist that you (go to when you) run out of things to do. So now it's like, 'OK, we didn't get the Album of the Year. Let's go (try again).' John Legend, Jon Brion, anyone named John, let's go."

Commenting, for his own part, on the role West had played in his phenomenal success, Legend acknowledged, "I think Kanye's success played an important role in setting me up for success. Of course, if my music sucked, Kanye's success still wouldn't have been enough. But, I think it did open some doors for me earlier than they would've been opened otherwise…People cared more about (my album) because he was attached to it and he was an 'it' artist at the time and still is, even more so now…So it got more attention than just the average R&B singer would have got."

Either way, critics were quick to recognize Legend on his own merits as a songwriter, even while acknowledging Kanye's platinum touch as a producer. It almost worked more in West's favor to play the background in critical commentary of Legend's debut LP under his collaboration with West, allowing the R&B star to stand on his own two feet, which most felt he did as a veteran, in spite of his newcomer status.

Rolling Stone Magazine LOVED Legend's debut, concluding that "for the past decade, R&B has tried to be as extravagant as the hip-hop that usurped its place. Kanye West protégé Legend has more modest aims. His brand of soul is mannered, even elegant. And he's got range: Two luscious odes to infidelity—'She Don't Have to Know' and 'Number One'—are followed by an equally convincing promise to not stray, 'I Can Change.' Best of all, 'Used to Love U' bears West's self-doubting stamp: 'Maybe, baby/Puffy, Jay-Z would all be better for you/'Cause all I could do is love you.'"

Vibe Magazine, meanwhile, proclaimed that "R&B the way it was meant to be—legendary…After playing a backup role to Kanye West on the omnipresent 'Jesus Walks,' John Legend begins his

own legacy with his major label debut, Get Lifted. Produced mostly by West and Legend, the album takes a soulful approach to R&B. Sonically touching all the bases, Legend recalls an era when less was more and talent triumphed over theatrics…By showcasing Legend's multiple talents, Get Lifted advances the kind of genre-pushing spirit that made D'Angelo's Brown Sugar so sweet. It's refreshing to hear a male vocalist who has enough talent to be more than a legend in his own mind."

"When someone hears your song and cries, then you're in touch and that's what matters. At that point, you feel like you've touched the sky."

Kanye West

Part 8
Late Registration

Out of his success, West found motivation to re-enter the studio to begin work on his highly-anticipated follow-up to 'College Dropout,' explaining that "this has inspired me...I want to top this last album. I want to do better. I'm inspired, I'm ready to write. I've been on the road for a long time, I'm ready to get back into the studio."

'Late Registration' might as well have been called 'PH D' in terms of the expectations people had for West's follow-up to the masterpiece that composed his debut, which were as advanced as West's sound surely was expected to be. For his own part, West admitted that "the pressure was on...The heat is on. But that's the joy of being under pressure, to go back and win that second championship...The ability to create and be creative is the reason why I think I can overcome the sophomore slump...Second albums, man, they're even scarier than first ones... I feel like after I finish this album, I was thinking about how can I come out with the

next one. How can I keep it up to the standard of quality that The College Dropout is?

And the whole point is to never change, you know? Never start talking about what you've done in the past. That's what I feel is wrong with rap. People rap so much about what they've done. Tupac for the most part rapped about what we are going through, what people are going through. And as long as I keep that in mind, I'll be able to always touch issues. There are so many issues—more issues in this world to bring up than the amount of music that I can make. So I'll never run out of ideas."

In terms of more broadly outlining surface or thematic contrasts between the lyrical material on College Dropout in contrast to Late Registration, West—an expert at the injection of pop culture analogies into his broader message—explained cleverly that "I felt like I was the rap Ben Stiller or the rap Dave Chappelle at one point, but now with this new album I am saying I am more the rap Steven Spielberg… I'm just getting real nice on the raps, so I write something and it is real nice, so like a week later I just want to rewrite because I'm crazy nice….I have been studying poetry, and I actually have had like tutors to help me play (more) with the words…The way the words make rhythms themselves, and I want to be able…to do more of that and that happened kind of late into the album…One thing that I like to do is use words that have never actually been used in a rap song before. I also like to take words that have negative connotations and show their real meaning. Like the word 'pop.' This is a pop album, but pop has a negative connotation if you're a 'real artist.' The title of The College Dropout—that's what that was…I want to…separate myself from just regular rap and make it more philosophical and stand the test of time, and always stay away from…cliché subject matters, and things that are only here for today and gone tomorrow. Make a piece of music that you…can place in a time capsule and it will represent whatever year it came out."

Of course, the deeper West got into the production of his sophomore opus, the more confident he grew in the project as it took shape, bolstering his self-assuredness to the point where he was talking louder and more boldly than he ever had previously—to the point where he'd written a check that he'd critically be ruined by, if he didn't cover creatively. I feel I could rhyme better than a lot of muthafuckers that have deals, but I feel like I can produce…I've got the potential to take it there…I didn't want to play it boring and safe. I also didn't want to innovate too much. Second albums, man, they're even scarier than first ones…(My goal with this album is to go) platinum…to have songs that are respected across the board, to have some sort of influence on the culture and to change the sound of music and inspire up-and-coming artists to go against the grain…It's got all these pop accolades, but it also really connected in the hood. It's what you attempt to do every time you walk into the studio…There's nothing that they would love more than me to come sub par so they could find something wrong…I'm not putting nothing out unless I can talk my shit. I want to give y'all something that y'all will remember."

One thing West was sure to do—in spite of the pressure he put on himself to raise the creative bar—was to reject any pressure from the higher-ups, spending over a year and $2 Million to make 'Late Registration.'

Explaining his philosophy on having the creative room to give his label the best product he could to guarantee maximum sales, West explained that "they were trying to rush this (one song) out and put it on a soundtrack, and I'm anti-'getting the music out.' Like, with 'The College Dropout', a lot of those songs took four, five months, a year to write. I made this (one) beat back in July, and throughout the whole Usher tour I would go back and sit in my room and just play the beat, like, a hundred times trying to figure out what I was gonna say. Each line is really important to me and I can't rush that process. I felt like the last album didn't sound as good as it could have because I had these deadlines, so this time

I'm gonna make sure that I put everything I want into the record before it comes out, and I can't give up a piece of my life to a soundtrack. This is a whole creation, 'Late Registration.' A lot of times people see that big buck, and I even got offered astronomical amounts. It's not about the money; it's about making the best record possible. And a lot of times you've got to stop the execs from being involved."

Musically, he elaborated to explain that, in broader terms, "the songs make sense though. Well, my songs (from Late Registration) are a part of an album set. I picture these songs like scenes in a movie. Now, how do I make this scene over here talk about some relationship and make it relate to this song that's talking about the roles in community and society?...Now, how do I make that relate to something else? How do I make things from this movie and make it something else? I can make a good song, a good single, but I have to think about my movement...(My) style (of sampling sped-up soul classics) has just been so oversaturated...But I never did that on purpose anyway. And then it just started to become a crutch...(On Late Registration), I figured out ways to chop it in a way where you can still get the soul out of it...I didn't want to play it boring and safe...I also didn't want to innovate too much."

To accomplish the latter, West enlisted a creative ally and co-producer in a move no one saw coming when he hired Jon Brion to co-helm the project. Perhaps best known as Fiona Apple's producer, West was a massive fan of Brion's production style, and out of the collaboration, hoped to elevate his own sound by broadening the influences as another creative mind interpreted them musically in the context of West's sound. "I just felt no one was doing that in hip-hop, no rapper has ever captured that sound and rapped on it. It's like, how many more sped-up soul samples do you want? We gotta push the envelope a little bit. And I always wanted to feel like I was rapping at the top of a mountain or something...Jon Brion...did 'Magnolia', 'Eternal Sunshine for the Spotless Mind', and Fiona Apple's ('Tidal.') He plays every instrument…Have you heard the level of genius that Jon Brion is? If you reference that, you will understand. That was me attempting to make something on the (highest) production level. I could only work up to what I knew. Now I know where it really comes from like the people that orchestrate the shit…When I listen to (Fiona's) shit, I hear similarities. I actually wanted to work with (Jon) so I could be like the rap version of (her). That was one of my main goals. The albums that inspired me for 'Late Registration' were (Fiona Apple's) first one, 'Tidal' and Portishead's 'Dummy', but especially (Fiona Apple's) lyrics and how (she) sing(s)…I (also) always loved…Fiona Apple's 'When the Pawn Hits' so much. It hit me in a way and I wanted to know, who got the drum sounding like that? Who went into these dark chords, these string arrangements? Who brought Fiona's pain to life? I needed someone that could bring my plight to life…(Jon Brion's) energy is so good to have while you're working on an album. He comes in, and he'll hear something that he likes and hit you with that…The sound is a little bit darker. We're kind of pushing the envelope with the music…We get a lot of that instrumentation cause I was really trying to push the envelope and show people where we can take it…(This is) the greatest meeting of creative musical minds."

For Jon Brion—who co-wrote with West, as well as arranged strings, and played keys and guitars among other instruments on the record—collaborating with West was apparently a matter of equal admiration and excitement, with the producer explaining that "I'm a fan of the guy. I've loved watching him work…I think there was a great deal in COMMON between us…Kanye is absolutely obsessed with wanting to make something really good…It was completely apparent that he was open to investigating new ideas…I was playing something on a track and he was completely psyched, and then he left after a few hours and said, 'I'll see you tomorrow.' When he hears something he likes, he knows it…He has vision, and when the guy makes quick, intuitive decisions, he just *has* it. I'd watch him take a rough track that I had worked on and completely stand it on its head in 10 minutes—and it's just *better*. It was mind-boggling…There are colors and ideas that make (the album) different from average hip-hop, but Kanye is already different from the average hip-hop guy. He's got this sense of pop record-making which is really solid, and he likes tracks with a lot of things going on in them—which is not necessarily COMMON for hip-hop. He was already barking up that tree…His last album wasn't just boasting, as is COMMON with rappers. He stayed on topic; he is focused on the songs. That's why I like working with artists like Fiona Apple and Aimee Mann…Some people who hear about this assume it's just total madness…But why not make the attempt to bridge as many gaps as possible?…This is definitely not just a hip-hop album…But it is also by no means overtly arty, or non-hip-hop. I don't think it's a weird record by any means."

In offering first-hand insight into West's songwriting and producing process for the album, Brion explains that "he came in with the basic samples and drum beats, and sometimes a verse of the raps. We're doing all sorts of things with real instruments…He will do his rap, and then sing a chorus, sing an octave above it, then come in and listen. He tells me, 'I need somebody with a reedy voice to do the top part and somebody with a huskier voice for the bottom part.' He starts mentioning people he has in mind. I said, 'You just wrote the chorus and you figured out mentally how it should be presented.' He thinks in frequency ranges. I can recognize when someone sees music architecturally, which is how I work. I see it as a spatial thing: left to right, front to back, up and down. It's animated and it's moving in real time. Kanye has that. He said, 'I see things in my head and they are complete and then I have to put it together in the recording.' He tries things out until it fits, until it sits where it is supposed to sit and everything has the correct emotional function. He has real instincts like any great record-maker…Kanye is the first person to make the connection on a purely sonic level. He noticed some sonic signposts. And his decisions are intuitive and not random. Once he was here, it freaked him out that I was playing parts-oriented stuff for the whole take rather than playing chords or noodling…When Kanye hears something he likes, he knows it…I would just lay out on any given song a bunch of different options of ways it would go. He'd be like, 'I like this, I like this and I like this.' I'd be like, 'Great, we'll focus on those things.' For me, it's easy to take any given piece and push it in a million different directions. It's not hard to do. What you need is the artist who has these visions of what they like and what they don't like and stand by it. I think he kind of got used to asking crazy things of me and me making them for him and then him deciding whether he wanted them or not…I'm fond of it all…I knew the last record, and I am incredibly impressed by his instincts."

An interesting component of the collaboration between West and Brion seemed to be how much their mutual talents fascinated one another, such that their time in the studio was a constant learning process. The result would be a lesson for the listener, but first for both producers in how to innovate expertise; how to open the creative mind to new things that would have appeared old or outdated sonically or instrumentally to anyone else but perhaps these two men in context of their goals for the album.

As Brion qualified the latter in terms of the results, he explained that "one of the reasons I collect old equipment is because of the way different artists react as they come into this unfamiliar environment. We get new sounds that are very, very interesting. They want to experiment, they start playing around and that's when I like to start recording…(We recorded at) Grand Master recording studios, famous for sessions with Ringo Starr, Billy Preston, Harry Nilsson and Beatles-related '70s-era stuff. I came in to do a little instrumental project, and Kanye came by the very next day. He brought along some Pro Tools files, but I didn't really know what he wanted to do. I introduced him to The Pile, which is what we

call this collection of instruments and old electronic gear...(In one example, Kanye) came up with a great part...when I set up a weird old early sampling keyboard, the 360 digital keyboard—the first commercially available sort of sample player. We are bringing out a lot of early '80s technology because he relates to the synths and drum machines...(Out of that), I discovered that he is a great drum programmer and great at manipulating samples. I introduced him to the Celeste and it blew his mind, and then to the Chamberlin. I said, 'Here is the original sampler, invented in 1946, and there's a tape player under every key, with recordings on this one of the Lawrence Welk Orchestra recorded in the late '50s.' I put my hand on the keys and you could see fire shooting out of his eyes, he was so excited. So here we are with the instrument collection, and we are following my obsession of making new sounds appear in a very organic way."

Continuing, and in the course offering further insight into West's real-time growth as a producer, as the stakes elevated approaching deadline for his follow-up LP, Brion observed that "what's interesting is that our tastes are similar, but not in specifically the records we listen to but what we listen for. Quality of experience. How it connects with the body. When there is a decisive change in the record to keep your interest up. All those little things are the intrinsic heart and soul of record-making. It's why Rick Rubin and Dr. Dre are the producers of their generation. I don't think anyone else is even close, (except perhaps Kanye). It is no accident that they have had careers nearly two decades long, consistently hitting the mark. They have a sense of what a record is supposed to be about and they bring that to the studio. With hip-hop , the notion is that you always have to have the latest 'thing.' But what's funny to me is that the sounds that everyone likes are coming off these old records. The sounds went through multiple tape generations before going to the mix and then to vinyl, and then the records were kicked around for 20 years before they were sampled. That's a lot of generations to have the EQ softened, for it to get grainy. But that's what works. Me with my piles of instruments, with knives and forks stabbed into them to keep them working—these crazy half-working instruments—actually help to make the sounds that hit the spinal chord in the way that Kanye wants. And, Kanye is loving it. I have an excited artist."

One thing West definitely seemed about the new material was excited, explaining that where hits were concerned, the album had plenty, in particular a song he had collaborated on with Jamie Fox, hot off his Oscar for portraying Ray Charles. Entitled 'Gold Digger', West explained the essence of why the song was a hit by identifying its "choruses and hooks. That's why the Black Eyed Peas' 'My Humps' is a killer. That song is just constant hooks all the way. See, people think a chorus is the only hook, but 'Gold Digger' has so many hooks in it. Jamie's intro, that's a hook. The drum intro, that's a hook. 'I ain't sayin' she a gold digger'; that's a hook.

The entire second verse is a hook: '18 years, 18 years.' That could be a chorus! 'We want prenup'; that's a hook. And the white-girl line? That's why I get the big bucks. That's bottom of the ninth, bases loaded, World Series. That's gold... It makes you think. That's a serious situation right there. Look how I broke down at the end , how niggas be getting rich and leaving their black girlfriend for a white girlfriend. That's not just a rap about money and girls. And I do it in such a charming way...'Gold Digger' is the quintessential Kanye West record."

Elaborating, Kanye's A&R rep Patrick Renyonds explained that "Jamie went in the booth and recorded a whole bunch of takes…The beginning, 'She takes my mon-eeee', was an ad lib. It was actually a lot dirtier. But after he recorded it, Jamie like, 'Y'all can't use that.' He was cursing on it." Another of West's collaborators, Maroon 5 front man Adam Levine, who sang on 'Heard 'Em Say', explained that working with West was "really a cool, organic process…Kanye's lyrics were beautiful."

Elaborating further, Kanye explained that "(Adam) came to the studio right after the Grammys and he sang the song and the melody fit perfect with it. He added something to it. It was just like the magic, the frosting on top. And that's one of those times that God is working in the studio with you."

Yet, another musical pairing that would have seemed wildly out of place, were it not for Brion and Levine's appearances on the album, was West's hook-up with guitarist/crooner Jon Mayer, who West chose to work with because " I was a fan of his music. He's one of those artists that, when I'm around white people, I can name, and it makes me seem like I really listen to white music." Mayer, for his part, explained the genesis of the collaboration as casual, wherein "I stopped by the studio just to say hello, and they said 'Kanye is in the studio.' So I said 'Great, I'd love to finally meet him.' He was with COMMON, playing some stuff. I remember I was sitting there and I raised my hand and said 'I can add to that.'…I raced back to my place, grabbed my amp and my guitar. When I hear something I can go on, and there's not a lot—as a guitar player—that's out right now that I can find a nice situation for. But I heard that and I was like 'I have got to put something on this.' The next day I (also) came back and did some vocals (for 'Bittersweet.')"

If West was trying to corner the pop market via his collaborations with mainstream superstars like Jon Mayer, Adam Levine, and Jon Brion among others who appeared on 'Late Registration', he succeeded when the album landed atop the Billboard Top 200 Album Chart in September, 2005, moving 860,000 copies in its first week of release, and quickly going triple platinum off the strength of the # 1 smash single 'Gold Digger', featuring Jamie Foxx. Critically, 'Late Registration' lived up to the expectations everyone had placed in it. The latter was true so much so for West that he declared on the outset of the 2006 Grammy Awards that "if I don't win Album of the Year, I'm gonna really have a problem with that...I can never talk myself out of [winning], you know why? Because I put in the work. I don't care if I jumped up and down right now on the couch like Tom Cruise. I don't care what I do, I don't care how much I stunt—you can never take away from the amount of work I put into it. So I don't wanna hear all of that politically correct stuff. You put the camera in front of me, I'm gonna tell you like this. I worked hard to get here. I put my love, I put my heart, I put my money (into Late Registration.) I'm $600,000 in the hole right now on that album and you tell me about being politically incorrect?...People love these songs...You talk to somebody whose grandmother just died and listens to 'Roses,' and you tell me about being politically incorrect. I'm talking about history. I never got five mics [top rating] in The Source, I never got five stars from Vibe. They said it's not a classic. So 'Jesus Walks' is not a classic? 'Roses' is not a classic? 'Gold Digger' wasn't song of the year? 'Oh, but Kanye, you can't say that.' Why? Who are you? I don't know you...I said I was the face of the Grammys last year. I'm 10 times that (this year)...Get your cameras ready. Two things: Do not let me get up on that stage and do not let me get up on that stage. Either way, we going crazy!..(The album) is really important not just because it was successful this year, but 10 years from now they'll look back at what it did for the game. The usage of strings, all types of instrumentation, the musicality of it, the fact that we sat and waited two weeks to rent a real harpsichord to put on 'Diamonds'—that's one instrument! Now let's take all the songs that were on there and add up the amount of work that went into it; this is the real thing. We put so much pain,

blood, sweat, tears, time and money into it, so for it to be nominated is great, but for it to win would be the seal of the work. It really needs that. It would be the first album in Grammy history that was all Rap that won for *Album Of The Year.*"

Needless to say, West won big at the 2006 Grammys, eclipsed only by U2 for 'Album of the Year', and won 3 Grammy Awards for Best Rap Solo Performance ("Gold Digger"), Best Rap Song (songwriting with D. Harris) ("Diamonds From Sierra Leone") and Best Rap Album (Late Registration), out of 10 overall nominations which also included nominated for Album of the Year (Late Registration), Record of the Year ("Gold Digger"), Best R&B Song (writing Alicia Keys' "Unbreakable" with Garry Glenn, Keys, and Harold Lily), and Best Rap/Song Collaboration ("They Say" with COMMON and John Legend from COMMON's LP, BE). Kanye was also nominated a second time in the Album of the Year for his production work on Mariah Carey's The Emancipation Of Mimi. West clearly wanted what he felt was certainly credit due from EVERYONE for an album that had dominated the latter half of 2005. Critics were in love with 'Late Registration', with Time Magazine declaring that "West is a master of samples and drum loops, and co-producer Brion can play anything with strings. Together they make one of the better-sounding rap records in history." Vibe Magazine, meanwhile, concluded that "when Kanye West strikes that right combination of social consciousness and street credibility, the message in his medium is magical…On the exhilaratingly original 'Diamonds From Sierra Leone', he's the first mainstream rapper to draw a connection between music industry ice and Africa's endemic political and economic crises…(Taking) his prodigious musicality to soaring new heights…(and) equipped with a grandiose vision and an expert ear, West experiments with darkly rendered marching-band drums, sweeping orchestral vistas… Late is also more thematically focused than The College Dropout. It's packed with big ideas about black power and hypocrisy and

populated with memorably drawn personalities…West wins when he keeps his ideals lofty. It's a thin line between commercial and conscious, between G.O.O.D. and bad, and that's bad meaning good." West's home paper, the Chicago Sun Times, for its part, praised "West's genius as a musical chef…(resting) in the ingredients he chooses, and in how he mixes them together in ways that seem fresh and unique." Regardless of the acclaim from critics—which was undeniably important to West—the rapper/producer seemed most interested in pleasing his fans, such that, at the end of the day, "with or without any accolades, whatever it is, the fact that people listen to this music and it's connected with people, the fact that you see fans crying in the audience — you can't tell me anything after that because there's so many places and establishments where people are out of touch…When someone hears your song and cries, then you're in touch and that's what matters. At that point, you feel like you've touched the sky."

Conclusion
Hip-hop Looks WESTward...

What more can anyone say about Kanye West, well… except Kanye West? His best press comes from his own mouth, and usually, he's right in one form or another no matter how provocative or controversial his comments are. He's almost always prompting or reacting to talk about himself, and therein, he ultimately sets the tone of almost anything that is reported on, editorialized about, or observed about him—be it musical, personal, commercial, and so forth. Because he also sets the tone commercially in terms of all things hip-hop, its fair to say that West has cornered a market in which—more or less—he has no truly viable competitors. As such, he has only himself to top—and his seemingly inevitable fear that he might fall off the top of his own game and mountain of commercial domination. That just might be enough for a man whose creative genius constantly challenges him, who rarely seems 100% happy with his own results, even when everyone around him is. West has all the talent and breeding to become the next Dr. Dre, and he very well may be on his way. He correctly predicted at the outset of 'Late Registration's release that his sound would "what music will be for the next four years at least," and looking in reflection on his potential to heavily shape the sound and direction of hip-hop , in one form or another', for perhaps years beyond the latter time frame, West reasoned that "I'm 28 years old and I've accomplished all these things."

Clearly feeling his talent, in the context of influence, was and would continue to be timeless—no matter its medium of application, as he boldly expressed via the sentiment that "the people talk about, 'Yo, you got this window, you got this window,' and naw, I don't think I have a window, I think I have a terrace. I don't think it's going to close like that because I'm still the best-dressed...So I think I can slowly and organically get into it and build it up, and make it something that's special and really respectable 'cause I'm going to design it. That's what I am more than anything—is a designer. I design my lifestyle. I design these tracks. I design raps. I design studios. Everyone always uses the word produce, yeah it's production, but it's still a design. Design hints at having some sort of taste...I am not talented for anything except the ability to learn...want to direct...I'm always thinking about stuff like, 'That would be dope in a movie,'...It's just like knowing how to rap or sing. You just experience it. Like I know a movie would just be like so extra challenging and I'd just have to study...And if I am really convinced by something, if it's something that really means a lot to me, then not only will I be able to learn how to do it to the point where I can be successful at it—but I will do it to the point where it pushes whatever that is, ahead of where it was before I got into it...I had to be a borderline lunatic to think that I could do what I've done. It's crazy what I've accomplished is crazy."

For an artist who started out his debut LP with the lines "Drug dealin' just to get by, stackin' money till it gets sky high, wasn't s'posed to make it past 25, the joke's on you we still alive, so throw your hands up in the sky, and sing 'We don't care what people say'," West came to the game to make a statement that would stamp a generation—he instead wound up defining one in terms that don't look to expire any time soon. In that context, this can't rightfully be titled as a 'conclusion', but rather an introduction to the next chapter of whatever Kanye West's wave of creative greatness is sure to be as the millennium rolls onto his beats and boundless artistic and commercial feats. If his perpetual greatness were suddenly to become stunted due to some radical shift in trends or times, West has said he "would probably try to spend a lot of time with my mother and my father, try to call all the people that I knew that I loved. Maybe try to write one last rap, do a song, draw pictures, write down a couple of video (treatments), write down all my ideas that I have that have not come out yet, and hope that maybe someone can expand on them when I'm not here."

In the context of finality as it pertains to his place in the annals of hip-hop , West is a true time traveler, as there's a good possibility time will never define West in terms of limitations in terms of popularity or relevance. Dipping back in time when he needs to remind hip-hop listeners where they come from through the sampling of a classic soul hook, West always reminds us of where we're heading in the same time with the translation of that sample into modern—and often futuristic—soundscapes which dominate radio and record sales. With a creative mind that operates in a constant state of reinvention, West perhaps fights to ensure he receives his due props in the present because he's ahead of us in understanding the impact his sound is having on one moment in terms of shaping the next. Whether in the studio or on stage, or video, radio, or whatever other medium of media he masters in spreading his message, West is at peace with one notion central in relevance to his greater legacy: that however history ends up recognizing him in time, "I know that if I were to die tonight, they would put my face on every cover and say I changed hip-hop . As long as you're here…they don't want to give you the credit."

Kanye West (The Early Years) Discography:

2002

November

▼ Kanye appeared on Jay-Z's LP The Blueprint 2: The Gift And The Curse with the track "The Bounce."

2004

▼ # 33 Singles Artist of the Year

January

▼ Kanye hit the Top 40 helping out Twista and Jamie Foxx with "Slow Jamz."

February

▼ Kanye released his debut LP The College Dropout.

▼ Kanye hit the Top 10 with Twista and Jamie Foxx with "Slow Jamz."

March

▼ Kanye hit the Top 40 "Through The Wire."

▼ Kanye appeared on Janet Jackson's LP Damita Jo with the track "My Baby."

April

▼ The College Dropout was certified platinum.

May

▼ Kanye hit the Top 40 with Syleena Johnson with "All Falls Down."

August

▼ Kanye was nominated for 6 MTV Video Music Awards including Best Male Video, Best Hip-Hop Video, Best New Artist, Breakthrough Video ("All Falls Down" with Syleena Johnson), Best R&B Video ("Talk About Our Love" with Brandy), and the MTV2 Award ("Slow Jamz" with Twista and Jamie Foxx). Kanye also performed at the ceremony.

▼ Kanye began touring as the opening act for Usher's tour.

October

▼ Kanye won 3 Source Awards for Album of the Year, Video of the Year ("Through The Wire"), and Breakthrough Artist.

November

▼ Kanye was nominated for 3 American Music Awards including Favorite Breakthrough Artist, Favorite Rap Male Artist, and Favorite Rap/ Hip-Hop Album. Kanye also performed at the ceremony.

December

    ▼ Kanye's The College Dropout was chosen by Rolling Stone magazine's critics as the best album of the year.

Kanye topped the Billboard Year-End Charts as the Top New Pop Artist, Top New R&B/Hip-Hop Artist, and Top Hot Rap Artist.

2005

    ▼ # 20 Singles Artist of the Year

January

    ▼ Kanye could be heard on the soundtrack to Coach Carter with "Wouldn't You Like To Ride."

February

    ▼ Kanye won 3 Grammy Awards for Best R&B Song (awarded to the songwriter) ("You Don't Know My Name" with Alicia Keys and Harold Lilly), Best Rap Song (awarded to the songwriter) ("Jesus Walks" with C. Smith), and Best Rap Album (The College Dropout), and was nominated for Album of the Year (The College Dropout), Song of the Year (awarded to the songwriter) ("Jesus Walks" with C. Smith), Best Rap/Sung Collaboration ("Slow Jamz" with Twista and Jamie Foxx and "All Falls Down" with Syleena Johnson), Best Rap Solo Performance ("Through The Wire"), and Best New Artist. Kanye performed at the ceremony.

March

    ▼ Kanye won a NAACP Image Award for Outstanding New Artist.

    ▼ The single "Jesus Walks" was certified gold.

May

    ▼ The single "All Falls Down" was certified gold.

July

▼ On July 2nd, Kanye performed in Philadelphia as part of the worldwide Live 8 concerts. The mission of the concerts was to raise awareness of the on-going poverty in Africa and to pressure the G8 leaders to take action by doubling aid, canceling debt, and delivering trade justice for Africa.

August

▼ The video for "Jesus Walks" won a MTV Video Music Award for Best Male Video and was nominated for Video of the Year and Best Hip-Hop Video. Kanye performed at the ceremony.

▼ Kanye released his next LP Late Registration.

September

▼ Kanye appeared on a live NBC benefit show to help the victims of Hurricane Katrina, and went off-script to give his feelings about the slow response by President Bush; "George Bush doesn't care about black people." West also targeted the media: "I hate the way they portray us in the media. If you see a black family, it says they're looting. See a white family, it says they're looking for food."

▼ Kanye hit the Top 40 with "Gold Digger."

▼ Kanye topped the Billboard 200 LP chart, Top R&B/Hip-Hop Albums chart for 3 weeks, and Top Rap Albums chart with Late Registration selling over 860,000 copies in the US its first week of release. The LP also topped the charts in Canada.

▼ Kanye topped the Billboard Hot 100 Singes chart, Pop 100 chart, Hot R&B/Hip-Hop Songs chart, Hot R&B/Hip-Hop Airplay chart, and Hot Digital Tracks chart with "Gold Digger."

▼ Kanye performed on Shelter From The Storm: A Concert For The Gulf Coast—a benefit program shown on all the major networks simultaneously to raise money for those affected by Hurricane Katrina.

▼ Kanye performed on ReAct Now: Music & Relief—a benefit program shown on music video channels to raise money for those affected by Hurricane Katrina.

▼ Late Registration was certified 2x platinum.

October

▼ Kanye performed on Saturday Night Live.

▼ Kanye hit the Top 10 and #1 for 2 weeks with "Gold Digger."

▼ Kanye topped the Billboard Pop 100 Airplay chart, Hot 100 Airplay chart, and Rhythmic Airplay chart with "Gold Digger."

▼ Kanye hit the Top 40 with "Heard 'Em Say."

November

▼ Kanye topped the Billboard Digital Songs chart with "Gold Digger."

▼ Kanye could be heard on the Hurricane Relief: Come Together Now compilation with "We Can Make It Better."

December

▼ Kanye had the #9 selling LP of 2005 with Late Registration selling over 2.4 million copies during the year.

2006

February

▼ Kanye won 3 Grammy Awards for Best Rap Solo Performance ("Gold Digger"), Best Rap Song (songwriting with D. Harris) ("Diamonds From Sierra Leone") and Best Rap Album (Late Registration), and was nominated for Album of the Year

(Late Registration), Record of the Year ("Gold Digger"), Best R&B Song (writing Alicia Keys' "Unbreakable" with Garry Glenn, Keys, and Harold Lily), and Best Rap/Sung Collaboration ("They Say" with COMMON and John Legend from COMMON's LP, Be). Kanye was also nominated a second time in the Album of the Year for his production work on Mariah Carey's The Emancipation Of Mimi. Kanye also performed at the ceremony.

▼ Kanye appeared on the cover of *Rolling Stone*.

▼ Kanye hit the Top 40 with "Touch The Sky."

March

▼ Kanye won a Soul Train Music Award for Best R&B/Soul or Rap Video ("Gold Digger").

About the Author

Nashville-based music biographer Jake Brown has published thirty books, including *AC/DC: in the Studio, Tom Waits: in the Studio, Heart: In the Studio* (authorized and co-written with Ann and Nancy Wilson), *Iron Maiden: in the Studio, Prince: In the Studio, Motorhead: In the Studio* (co-written with Lemmy Kilmister), *Rick Rubin: In the Studio, Dr. Dre: In the Studio, Suge Knight: The Rise, Fall and Rise of Death Row Records, 50 Cent: No Holds Barred, Biggie Smalls: Ready to Die, Tupac: In the Studio* (authorized by the estate), as well as titles on *Kanye West, R. Kelly, Jay-Z, the Black Eyed Peas*, and other titles including *Red Hot Chili Peppers: In the Studio, Motley Crue: In the Studio, Alice in Chains: In the Studio, Meat Puppets: In the Studio* (co-written with Curt and Cris Kirkwood), *Tori Amos: in the Studio*, and *Third Eye Blind: in the Studio* (authorized).

Brown is also the co-author of founding Guns N' Roses guitarist *Tracii Guns'* authorized memoir, and a featured author in late funk pioneer Rick James' autobiography, *Memoirs of Rick James: Confessions of a Super Freak*, is the co-author of *What the Hell Was I Thinking?!* by retired adult film star Jasmin St. Claire and co-author of the legendary Judah boxing family's forthcoming authorized autobiography. In February 2008, Brown appeared as the official biographer of record on Fuse TV's Live Through This: Nikki Sixx TV special and in November, 2010, appeared as biographer of record on Bloomberg TV's 'Game Changers' Jay Z special. Brown has received additional press in national publications including *USA TODAY*, MTV.com, *The New York Post, Vibe, NPR, Billboard, Revolver*, and *Publishers Weekly* among many others. Brown was recently nominated alongside Lemmy Kilmister for the 2010 Association for Recorded Sound Collections Awards in the category of Excellence in Historical Recorded Sound Research. Brown is also owner of the hard rock label Versailles Records, distributed nationally by Big Daddy Music/MVD Distribution and celebrating a decade + in business this year.

ORDER FORM

WWW.AMBERBOOKS.COM

Fax Orders: 480-283-0991 / Telephone Orders: 602-743-7211
Postal Orders: Send Checks & Money Orders Payable to:
  Amber Books
  1334 E. Chandler Blvd., Suite 5-D67, Phoenix, AZ 85048
Online Orders: E-mail: Amberbk@aol.com

_____*Beyoncé Before the Legend,* ISBN #: 978-1-937269-42-5, $12.00
_____*Kanye West Before the Legend,* ISBN #: 978-1-937269-40-1, $15.00
_____*Nicki Minaj: The Woman Who Stole the World,* ISBN #: 978-1-937269-30-2, $12.00
_____*Eminem & The Detroit Rap Scene,* ISBN#: 978-1-937269-26-5, $15.00
_____*Too Young to Die, Too Old to Live: The Amy Winehouse Story,* ISBN#: 978-1-937269-28-9, $15.00
_____*Lady Gaga: Born to Be Free,* ISBN#: 978-1-937269-24-1, $15.00
_____*Lil Wayne: An Unauthorized Biography,* ISBN#: 978-0-9824922-3-9, $15.00
_____*Black Eyed Peas: Unauthorized Biography,* ISBN#: 978-0-9790976-4-5, $16.95
_____*Red Hot Chili Peppers: In the Studio,* ISBN #: 978-0-9790976-5-2, $16.95
_____*Dr. Dre In the Studio,* ISBN#: 0-9767735-5-4, $16.95
_____*Tupac Shakur—(2Pac) In The Studio,* ISBN#: 0-9767735-0-3, $16.95
_____*Jay-Z…and the Roc-A-Fella Dynasty,* ISBN#: 0-9749779-1-8, $16.95
_____*Ready to Die: Notorious B.I.G.,* ISBN#: 0-9749779-3-4, $16.95
_____*Suge Knight: The Rise, Fall, and Rise of Death Row Records,* ISBN#: 0-9702224-7-5, $21.95
_____*50 Cent: No Holds Barred,* ISBN#: 0-9767735-2-X, $16.95
_____*Aaliyah—An R&B Princess in Words and Pictures,* ISBN#: 0-9702224-3-2, $10.95
_____*You Forgot About Dre: Dr. Dre & Eminem,* ISBN#: 0-9702224-9-1, $10.95
_____*Michael Jackson: The King of Pop,* ISBN#: 0-9749779-0-X, $29.95

Name:_____

Company Name:_____

Address:_____

City:_____State:_____Zip:_____

Telephone: (____) _____E-mail:_____

For Bulk Rates Call: **480-460-1660**   **ORDER NOW**

Beyoncé	$12.00	❏ Check ❏ Money Order ❏ Cashiers Check
Kanye West	$15.00	❏ Credit Card: ❏ MC ❏ Visa ❏ Amex ❏ Discover
Eminem	$15.00	
The Amy Winehouse Story	$15.00	
Lady Gaga	$15.00	CC#_____
Nicki Minaj	$12.00	Expiration Date:_____
Lil Wayne: An Unauthorized Biography	$15.00	**Payable to:**
Black Eyed Peas	$16.95	Amber Books
Red Hot Chili Peppers	$16.95	1334 E. Chandler Blvd., Suite 5-D67
Dr. Dre in the Studio	$16.95	Phoenix, AZ 85048
Tupac Shakur	$16.95	
Jay-Z…	$16.95	**Shipping:** $5.00 per book. Allow 7 days for delivery.
Ready to Die: Notorious B.I.G.,	$16.95	
Suge Knight:	$21.95	**Total enclosed: $_____**
50 Cent: No Holds Barred,	$16.95	
Aaliyah—An R&B Princess	$10.95	
Dr. Dre & Eminem	$10.95	
Michael Jackson: The King of Pop	$29.95	